the punctured thumb

or, cactus and other succulents

GEORGE ASHLEY

DRAWINGS BY MAGGIE BAYLIS

**101 PRODUCTIONS
SAN FRANCISCO**

Printed and bound in the United States of America.

Distributed to the book trade in the United States
by Charles Scribner's Sons

Published by 101 Productions
834 Mission Street
San Francisco, California 94103

Library of Congress Cataloging in Publication Data

Ashley, George, 1930-
    The punctured thumb.

    Includes index.
    1. Cactus.   2. Succulent plants.   I. Title.
SB438.A73   635.9'55   77-21212
ISBN 0-89286-124-X pbk.

contents

Introduction 5

I Natural Beginnings 7
Some Reasons Why Succulents Should Be Our Favorite Plants 9
Shaking the Family Tree: Cactus and Other Succulents 15
The Name of the Game is Botany 26

II Indoor Plants 41
The Well Adjusted 43
The Fair-Haired Boys: Cactus 65
The Fair-Haired Boys: Succulents 75
The Tolerant Classics: The Rosette Form 81
The Genus Opuntia 91
The Ferocious 97
The Minis 103
The Granddaddy of Them All 107
The Commoners 110
The Crazies 113
The Epiphytes 121

III Culture 127
From the Bottom of the Pot Up 129

Mail-Order Source List 164

Index 165

DEDICATION

For the lady who, many years ago, was my high school botany teacher. She probably hoped for a more scholarly work . . . until she remembers that she gave me a D— on my final semester test.

This book is also dedicated to, and written for, people who wander through the cactus/succulent world feeling a little bewildered by it all, as well as for those who don't know a cactus from a castanet, up to and including those who have managed to kill off every succulent in the neighborhood by merely being in the same vicinity.

introduction

My mother was a cactus freak. My first word was "Ouch!"; the second also had four letters. Our family kitchen was, cactorically speaking, a wonderland. A goodly assortment of other succulents lived there, too, and to say that I lived, breathed and ate them is no exaggeration. A Burro's-Tail dangled into my oatmeal, and an Old Man cactus shed on my plate, until one day in a fit of indignation I shaved it with my father's razor. Consequently I became one of the few people who has ever seen an Old Man cactus in the nude, a fact that did not endear me to my parents or, for that matter, to the cactus.

There were succulent plants on the windowsills, on the shelves around the sink and at the ends of the cupboards, and on the table. You made no fast moves in the kitchen. I remember a cactus with spines long enough to hang a dish towel on, and a snaky-looking affair which crept around on a corner shelf and, according to my mother, had flowers of a unique smell. Whenever it bloomed, my father would glower and announce that a dead rat had fallen down between the walls. It was *that* kind of unique!

As I grew older, we inspected tropical succulents, foraged the deserts, paid homage to Luther Burbank's thornless opuntia in Santa Rosa and continued to fight a losing battle in the kitchen.

Cactus? Succulents? I've been there, from A to Z, from aloe to zygocactus. And on the way I've met the rest of the alphabet.

THE BIRTH OF A BOOK AND ITS RESEARCH

When it was suggested to me that I do a cactus book I ruminated about my past experiences for three days. Then I sobered up and wondered what I had in the way of solid factual material. I looked in my files ("files" is a term I use for the beer carton on the floor under my desk) and found something that made *War and Peace* look like a short story. It turned out to be my notes on *A Cactus is a Succulent, but Succulents Aren't Necessarily Cactaceous—Simplified.* I also seemed to have collected information on a motley assortment of related subjects—culture, potting, propagating, etc.—plus some historical data on how to use cactus spines to suture wounds, with which I wish I

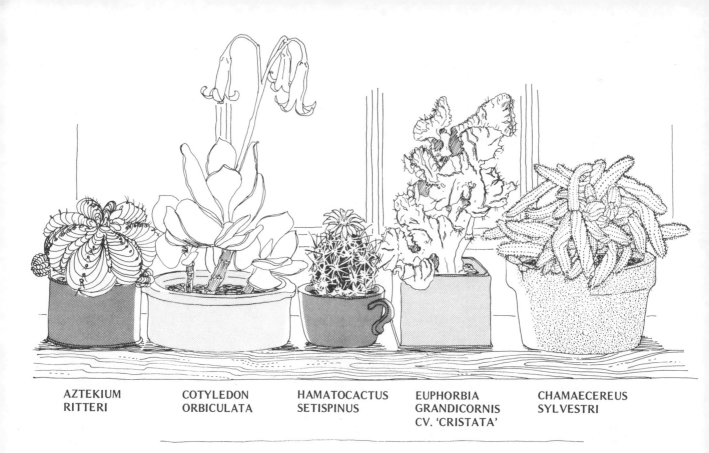

AZTEKIUM
RITTERI

COTYLEDON
ORBICULATA

HAMATOCACTUS
SETISPINUS

EUPHORBIA
GRANDICORNIS
CV. 'CRISTATA'

CHAMAECEREUS
SYLVESTRI

hadn't bothered. What did bother me were those "simplified" cactus/succulent notes. They were too complicated! Could there be an easier way?

I think this is the proper place to air my pet peeve: authors of layman's general information books who automatically assume you are so well acquainted with the nomenclature and scientific background of their subject that they don't bother to explain anything in words of less than six syllables. If he or she tells me facts I already know, that's ok; I don't mind reviewing. But I do resent being made to feel I am a nitwit because I don't understand the first sentence.

In making the language as simple and uncomplicated as possible, it is not my intention to insult the intelligence of anyone. If I simplify it is with good reason; when I get too scientifically involved I can't grasp what I'm writing about. And it's really humiliating not to understand a book you wrote yourself!

Although I may poke fun at botanists and taxonomists, I fully appreciate the work they are doing; it is an unbelievably frustrating and complex job. But, along with horticulturists and experienced amateur gardeners, they know the value of a sense of humor.

When trying to cope with Mother Nature, one must either learn to laugh or go mad. I've made my choice.

I NATURAL BEGINNINGS

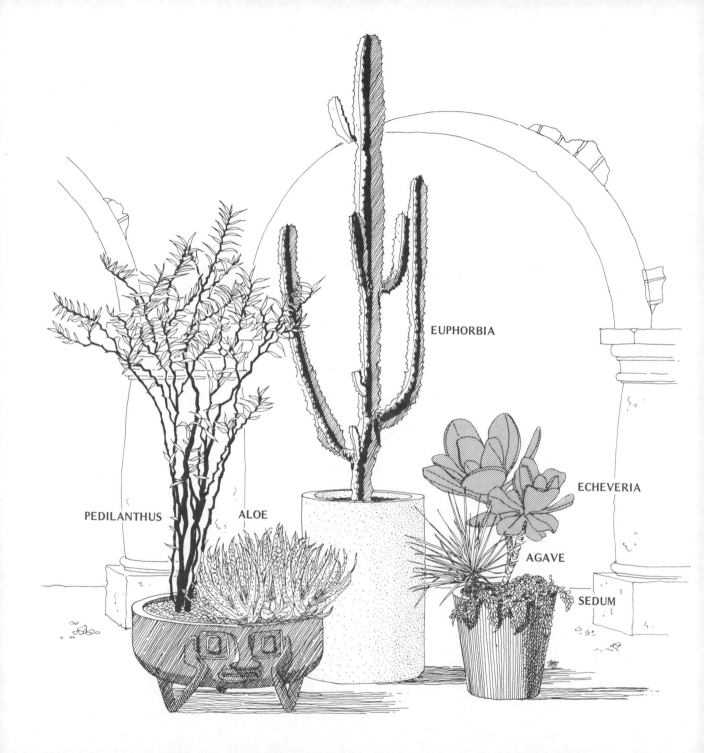

EUPHORBIA

PEDILANTHUS   ALOE

ECHEVERIA

AGAVE

SEDUM

some reasons why succulents should be our favorite plants

HUMIDITY? WHO NEEDS IT?

One of the best reasons for growing succulents is their easy culture, and one of the best points of that culture is that they are quite content to live in the relatively dry air of our homes . . . and in most homes the air is relative to Death Valley.

If you can identify with any one of the following situations, you have an ideal place to grow cactus and/or the other succulents. If you can identify with *all* of them, run for your life! Your house may blow up at any second from spontaneous combustion!

• A deep breath shrivels your sinus cavities and chips your lungs.

• There is so much static buildup in the rug that when you switch on a lamp, you light up before it does.

• After a week in the parlor, a Maidenhair fern looks like a dried arrangement.

• Somebody admires your tweed carpeting and then they find out the tweedy spots are dehydrated paint flakes from the ceiling.

• Friends with rheumatism who can't afford to go to Arizona for the winter make prolonged visits to your house.

Think of it! There really are plants that like this type of atmosphere. Prefer it, in fact. No more trays of wet gravel, no humidifiers to buy, no misting, spritzing or spraying, and no more dripping leaves, or dropping ones either. Humidity? Let someone else worry about it.

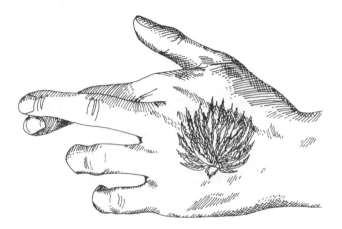

DON'T BE FLIMFLAMMED

Cactus culture is easy, but beware of the vicious rumor going around that cactus are completely care free. Not true! They do not thrive on neglect; nothing does, including you and me. While their care is not as complex, nor as time consuming as it is for other kinds of plants, they are not something you stick in a pot, dribble a little water on once a month and ignore the rest of the time. If you want something you can ignore, try your phone bill. People have plants because they want to pay attention to them, a little or a lot, depending on the person. If you just want something to balance one end of the front hall, fill the space in an empty corner or match the kitchen curtains, forget plants. Buy a vase.

Another nice thing about cactus: Failures are as scarce as white marigolds. Cactus are good for the ego. Of course if you are absolutely intent on destroying a succulent of any kind, it is easily done. Overwater it!

NO, YOU DON'T NEED
ONE MORE FOR THE ROAD

There was a time when cactus fanciers were accused of not playing with a full deck. Then somebody finally noticed that these odd people remained calm and cool while other green-growers were rushing madly around with their watering cans. These cactus folk just might know something. They did. And it's one more vote in favor of cactus culture. You don't have to be constantly watering the little beggars.

No, you can't take a four-month camel tour of Afghanistan and leave your cactus unattended, and still expect them to be alive and well when you get back. Some of them may be alive—they are tough —but they definitely will not be well. But when the world is too much with you and you'd like to flop down with a cold cloth on your head, say for a week or so, a cactus will understand. Leafy plants are not as magnanimous and tend to get sulky if even temporarily ignored.

SIT! AND STAY!

Besides being easy to grow, cactus are reliable and relaxing. What do I mean by that? Well, a cactus won't creep around the kitchen window, take off across the ceiling, go through the china cabinet and shoot out the back door. An ivy plant did this to me once and I simply don't trust it any more—very unreliable.

Cactus do not need to be pinched back, pruned off, strung up or tied down. They are not sneaky. They do what they are supposed to do, and they do it at a dignified pace. You will never, never come back from a weekend at the beach and find that a cactus has permanently attached itself to the dining room curtain rod, which is something a Passion vine will do at the turn of a back.

Some of the other succulents can move pretty fast, but as a rule they are all above such crass behavior. Possibly we could learn something from their "take it easy" attitude. Why, indeed, must we always be in such a hurry? Could be a few of these relaxed plants around the house would remind us to slow down.

Solid and reliable. No big surprises. Who needs them? We get surprises from our children, from the tax people, and occasionally from certain plumbing fixtures. We don't need surprises from our plants.

Cactus *flowers* do come as a surprise to some people though, as they are among the most beautiful in the plant kingdom. The colors are clear and bright, with a silky sheen; some are almost luminescent and many of them are perfumed. The structure of the bloom is a geometric wonder in itself.

BUG OFF!

Another plus: Succulents are not a choice item on the "Preferred Dinners for Bugs" menu. They do have some insect appeal of course, but the appeal is limited. They are *nearly* a "no bug's land" when compared to other plants, and the few insects that might set up light housekeeping are of the common, easy-to-control types. Nothing exotic. No beady-eyed bug with 13 legs, curb feelers and a racing stripe is going to eat your plants down to a stump and then finish off his meal by picking his teeth with a cactus spine.

Diseases? Only one of any magnitude—rot. And if your succulents get a terminal case of rot, you probably brought it on yourself by being heavy-handed with the watering can.

DON'T BELIEVE CACTUS ARE DULL!

Some people—why shilly-shally—*most* people think cactus are dull. On a scale of one to 100, they rate cactus somewhere between one and two. To them cactus are just greenish spiny lumps content to sit around and collect dust. Don't you believe it!

Cactus are peculiar. They are fleshy, sometimes flashy and often appealingly grotesque. They are moisture-hoarding, prickly, thick-skinned, slow-moving individuals who relish lazing in the summer sun. They like inactive winters, short naps and loose surroundings. They also take kindly to being potted. (By the merest coincidence, this also happens to be a fairly accurate description of my brother-in-law.)

The cactus family has about 2000 species, a seemingly endless number of varieties, and hybrids galore. They can't all be greenish spiny lumps! Somewhere in those vast numbers there must be something for you. But a word of warning (and no pun intended): Once you get hooked on cactus it is very difficult to keep from adding "just one more." It's like eating salted peanuts; one is invariably followed by another ... and another ... and ... !

Buy a fat little Pincushion cactus and the first thing you know you'll *have* to have one of the hairy kinds, one of those cactus so hirsute it looks like something you'd snap a leash on and take for a walk. Or you'll become fascinated with a big beastly thing with spines so menacing you're afraid to approach it without a whip and a chair. Could be you'll crave a cactus that is tall and stately and disdainfully elegant. Or maybe you'll fall for a little one that looks like an enraged Brillo pad.

Sure, you may have to adjust your idea of house plantery in order to fully appreciate them, but once you get the hang of it, look out! By the time you get control of yourself in the cactus department, you will have found out about all the other succulents, and nowhere else will you find plants as diverse, as different, as beguiling. Some are not for the timid and some are definitely a challenge, but none of them can be classified as ho-hum plants.

There are succulents with strange blooms right out of a science-fiction movie, or else the whole plant is so weird that when you tell friends it came from Mars, they believe you. Others imitate pebbles so successfully visitors will stop to admire your quaint rock collection. There are crazy succulents that look like something left over from an explosion in a gear and sprocket factory. Some have more dangling parts than a Victorian lampshade, and some are neatly compact, almost mathematically precise.

Who can resist? Not me! And a trip through a good cactus/succulent nursery or retail house will convince you, too. As tempting bait, mail-order catalogs aren't too shabby either. (If they were in color, there wouldn't be a dry eye in the house.)

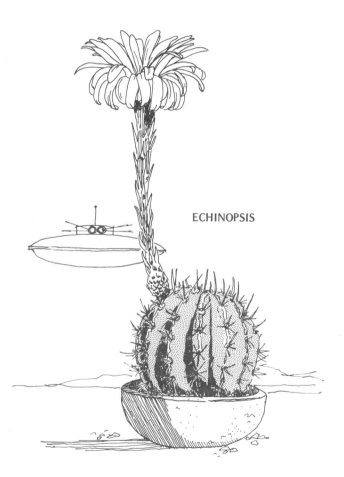

ECHINOPSIS

13

NO ROMANCE?

Do I hear a skeptical voice? "Ok, cactus aren't dull, but they have no romance in their fat, little bodies."

I can't imagine a more misguided romantic than Madame Bovary, but if cactus turned her on, that's good enough for me. Seems both Emma Bovary and her lover had windowsill collections of cactus, and they lovingly gazed out at each other while tending their respective pots. Now that's what I call pretty heady stuff! Unfortunately, in my neighborhood such carryings on would probably only reduce property values.

LAST, BUT NOT LEAST

As much as I like my other plants, and I am fond of them, there are times when the profusion of leaves, stems, twigs and branches becomes too ... uh, profuse. At those times I find it very relaxing to rest my tired eyes on the quiet, clean lines of cactus plants. They are clearly defined pieces of living sculpture. Like Mt. Everest, they are *there.* Solid and determined and substantial.

The same can be said for most of the other succulents. Few of them are the least bit giddy. Perverse, maybe, but not giddy.

ASTROPHYTUM
CAPRICORNE

CORYPHANTHA
CLAVATA

Mme Bovary

14

shaking the family tree: cactus and other succulents

Other succulents? What's the difference? Who is what? And why? Those of you who already know the answers can skip the following fairy tale, although it might be interesting for you to see just how far some people will go to make their point.

THE SAGA OF THE DROUGHT LOVERS

Once upon a time, there were some very special creatures, whose ancestors had discovered how to make one big drink of water supply their bodily needs for a much longer time than was possible for other creatures. The ability to do this wonderful thing was refined and perfected, and passed along to future generations. Smaller pores to cut down on perspiration were inherited, and thicker skins, and best of all, special cells and tissues for storing moisture. After all, they could hardly be expected to carry the extra water in their stomachs; they would have sloshed when they walked. Fact is, though, they refined and perfected themselves right into a corner, and finally reached the stage

where they *couldn't* drink very often and stay healthy. Worse yet, somebody forgot to equip them with a "No thanks, I'll wait for the next round" response. They couldn't pass up a drink! When there was water around, they drank—soaked it up like blotters whether they needed it or not. The results were dire: too much water in their systems and they turned into slush. It was a ghastly way to go, and they became mighty particular about which neighborhoods they moved into.

So it came to pass that these creatures had only one thing in common. It was not race or creed or color, and not geographical location, as they were scattered here and there all over the world. Other than looking a little bloated, they didn't even resemble one another. They were as diverse a group as you could find anywhere, and only the fact that they lived where water was scarce was common to them all. Maybe rain fell seasonally and they had to store up for the dry spell, or maybe there just wasn't much water at any time of the year. At any rate, these special creatures were able to beat the system and make do with what water they could get, when they could get it, and they did it very successfully.

Then one day they decided they needed a name for their group. Everyone did concede to that much; they were a *special* group. Being a completely unscientific type of creature, they quite logically thought up a very simple name: Drought Lovers.

In one particular area of the world, and it was a big one, some of the Drought Lovers noticed that they had another common physical characteristic. Through evolution they had added a rather odd thing which was different from the Drought Lovers in Europe and Asia and Africa, or any place else. In North and South America the Drought Lovers' hair grew funny; they had these queer hair follicles. A poll was taken and after the usual red tape, it was found that every last one of the Funny-haired Americans was related. Truly related; a family in fact. It was quite an event.

For a while they were content to keep calling themselves Drought Lovers, but pride got the better of them and they decided they wanted a name all their own, a family name. Again, it seemed logical to pick a name that was descriptive and that's just what they did. Because of their funny follicles they called themselves Thistle Heads. Naturally, the Thistle Heads were still part of the Drought Lovers group, but the Drought Lovers from other parts of the world who had normal hair could never belong to the Thistle Head family . . . and what's more they probably didn't want to. But as soon as they heard that their American cousins had given themselves a high falutin' last name, they wanted one, too. So, they took a survey.

There was quite a flurry when they found out that some of them couldn't drum up an exclusive family name; part of them, the survey revealed, were already related to a number of non-Drought Lover families. After some confusion they finally sorted themselves out and each Drought Lover, Thistle Heads and non-Thistle Heads alike, soon had a family to belong to and a name to go with it. Of course, as a scientific name, Drought Lovers was much too easy to remember and pronounce, so botanists gave the entire group a better one. After much research, deep study and mumbling, they thought of a remarkably suitable new name— Xerophytes.

Shortly afterward, a botany student, who wanted to be on top of things, asked his professor what this new name, Xerophytes, meant. The professor looked at him like he was the village idiot and said, "It means Drought Lovers." And right then and there the student knew it wasn't going to be easy; only the plants were going to live happily ever after.

Now, for those of you who are still with me, the point is, botanically speaking, that Drought Lovers are the succulent group and Thistle Heads

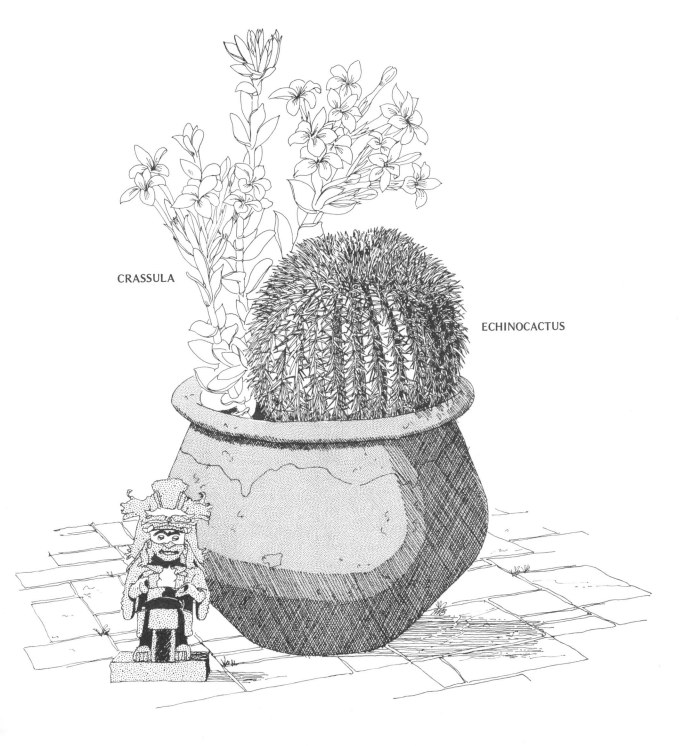

CRASSULA

ECHINOCACTUS

are the cactus family. This leads us to the amazing conclusion that all cactus are succulents, but not all succulents are cactus.

Like people, lots of plants do have a bloated relative or two hanging around cluttering up the family tree. The word succulent is from the Latin *succus*, meaning juicy, and many plant families include a succulent member. The lily family, for example, and the milkweed, amaryllis and spurge families. Some succulents have their own family, like the crassulas, the mesembs and the cactus.

The legal name of the cactus family is *Cactaceae*. (The family name always ends like that—in *aceae*—for any plant.) Cactus is a shortened form of the word melocactus (melonthistle) and it comes from the Greek *kaktos*, meaning prickly. The funny hair follicles? On a cactus they are called areoles, and areoles, not spines, are what make a cactus a cactus. No other plant has them. And if you're wondering what an areole is, we will get to them very shortly.

Now, if you read the fairy tale again, substituting the word plants for creatures, succulents for Drought Lovers, and cactus for Thistle Heads, it really sounds quite sensible.

No, I guess it doesn't.

NATURAL HISTORY
OF THE CACTUS FAMILY

Knowing a little about plants in their natural state is not an absolute necessity, but it does help us to understand what they expect in the way of care, and what we can expect in return for our ministrations. If cactus/succulent culture is different from that of other plants, maybe we ought to learn why it is. And how it got that way.

If you were trying to housebreak a hippopotamus, it would certainly be to your mutual advantage to know how it is fed, watered and potty-trained in the wild. How many papers are you *really* going to have to put down? Will it settle for a light lunch on Sundays? How long before it outgrows the bathtub? I'm sure you'd find out . . . before you both were at wit's end. Why not give plants the same break? Especially cactus. They have had a very hard time of it.

The ancestors of the cactus family probably started out in the jungles, then, adapting as they went, spread out into the drier areas. Or possibly the jungle moved out from under them through climatic changes; the earth was rather twitchy in those days. Whichever way it happened these plants underwent many changes, and these changes didn't just happen. The plants had to work at it.

Cactus, along with other succulent plants, re-designed the whole structure of plant life to suit themselves. Nobody before or since has gone to that much trouble. If nothing else, you have to respect what they did, whether you are a fancier or not: While other plants were content to grow and be pretty and wastefully prodigal, the succulents got right down to the basics of survival . . . without frivolities. It was the biggest do-it-yourself project on record.

When the ancestors left their warm jungle Eden they made a few fast adaptations, then they paused to ponder their situation. Some of them decided they didn't like it out there in the open; it was too exposed and too dry. It wasn't so much that the drinks were served few and far between, it was standing around in the hot sun waiting for them that got them down. So they sneaked back into the jungle and parked themselves on trees and logs, having already formed the habit of not wanting their feet in soggy soil.

Meanwhile, the rest of the family was left out there panting in the desert, trying to figure out what to do next. The only answer seemed to be that they must evolve into nothing more than a completely efficient plumbing system. In that respect they could no longer afford leaves!

A leafy plant has about 100 times the surface area of a barrel cactus of equal weight, and loses moisture close to 6,000 times faster. Leaves are a luxury. While other succulents pruned away the extra parts, some reducing themselves to the point where they were nothing but tiny green bumps which eventually became known by the inglorious name of "living rocks," the cactus family showed a little more imagination.

Of course they couldn't just do away with their leaves, not and stay alive (leaves manufacture food for the plant through a process called photosynthesis), so the stems and branches, green with chlorophyll, took over the job. That's why the mutant white, yellow and red cactus sold as oddities have to be grafted onto a green chlorophyll-

producing understock. But having the body of the cactus doing the work of its lost leaves wasn't enough in the water conservation department, so the development of a thick, waxy-finished skin was next on the agenda. The addition of spines and hair further cut down on moisture loss by casting a little shade, reflecting heat and insulating the stem surface. Spines and hair also made the plant better able to withstand the threat of evaporation from drying winds, and the possibility of extinction from hungry animals.

By growing in forms with ribs and tubercles, cactus presented a smaller exposed area for the elements to blast away at. These ridges and grooves could also contract or expand to accommodate the plant's water supply ... and the ridges threw a ribbon of shade into the grooves. Every little bit helped. Many cactus even have dished-in tops to protect the tender growing parts from wind and too much sun.

All these specialties were still not enough, so the cactus began refining the only thing they had left to work with on their exteriors: the *stomata* (Greek, for little mouths). Each stoma has two bean-shaped cells, like lips, one on each side of it. When these two cells are supplied with water they swell up and pull apart, leaving the stoma open to carry out photosynthesis. You can bet that if a cactus isn't well supplied with water, these two cells aren't either, and during hot dry spells when the cells are not swollen the stomata close up shop to conserve moisture. Naturally there is some water loss even then, which is a good thing in the long run; without some transpiration life processes would stop. It would be like plugging your nose and mouth completely to conserve air!

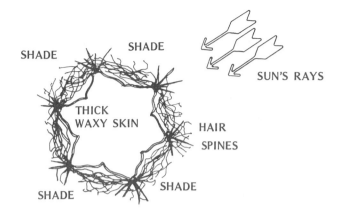

SECTION SHOWING RIBS

Besides being able to open and close, the cactus stomata don't miss any other tricks. They are countersunk below the surface of the plant in grooves or pits for added protection. They are often guarded by hairs or half plugged with a waxy substance, sometimes both. Cactus/succulent stomata are smaller than those of other plants and they are on the underside of any flat leaf-like structure the succulent might have, as opposed to the stomata of other plants being on top of the leaf. Usually stomata are open in the daytime and closed at night, but cactus have switched that around too: closed days, open nights.

With the outside remodeling job finished, our wily cactus turned to fixing up the inside. Tissues to retain water were developed and a mucus-like substance to thicken and bind the water was manufactured. They found out right away that a glutinous sticky liquid does not evaporate as fast as plain, thin water. This is the stuff that thirsty travelers are supposed to drink, and it has been done. While it's true enough that you can sustain yourself on the bitter, thick liquid squeezed from

21

the pulp of a barrel cactus, it helps if you are really, quite literally dying of thirst. As a casual refreshment it will never replace a mint julep.

Having pulpy insides worked fine for short, round cactus, but the tall columnar giants couldn't support their height, weight or branches with an interior that was nothing but wet glop. Another refinement was in the offing: An interior framework of flexible woody ribs provided the needed support. On dead and partially decomposed columnar cactus these ribs stick up as skeletal remains. Indians used them for firewood and building material, real wood being in short supply.

With the inside and outside completely overhauled to suit its environment, about the only thing left for the cactus to refurbish was its roots.

Cactus root systems are usually enormous in relation to the size of the plant. They may radiate some 40 to 50 feet around a large specimen. The roots are close to the surface of the ground, to catch rain quickly before it either evaporates or sinks right past them through the porous soil. They also are often close enough to the desert floor to collect morning dew. Cactus roots are covered with a corky material so they can soak up every drop of water available, and the same corky stuff insulates the root system against moisture loss during periods of drought and protects it from the high temperatures of the ground surface. The efficiency of a cactus is downright frightening.

Other succulents are just as efficient, more so in some cases. A few of the South African members contain up to 95 percent of their total weight in water. Some of these are called "window" plants because they bury themselves in the soil to escape the scorching sun, exposing only the translucent tips of their leaves. If it wasn't for the sake of photosynthesis they probably wouldn't come out at all. At that, they have provided themselves with a filter of crystalline material to reduce light intensity. Homegrown, built-in sunglasses if you will!

Some of the succulents have taproots, but as a rule these are used for anchoring purposes and not for moisture gathering. Others, like the yucca and Night-blooming cereus, have bulbous roots which store water for the plant as the leaves are not capable of housing an adequate supply. Succulent plants with thinner, or leafy-type, stems are more inclined to have tuberous roots. They have to keep their water supply someplace!

UNNATURAL HISTORY—A DIGRESSION

This title always perks up a certain contingent (and you know who you are). Nevertheless, strange things have happened, and are happening, in the succulent segment of plant life.

OVERT Serious botanical studies began in Europe and England, even for the native American plants. It seems we were too busy fighting the Establishment, the elements and each other, to get to the niceties of cactus literature. The first written reference to cactus was made in the mid-16th century and it was about their edible fruits and medicinal properties.

For a long time there was a great deal of balderdash about the magical uses, good and bad, of the cactus, all of which probably stemmed from the witnessing of, or participating in, a peyote party. Cactus spines, it was said, were poisonous and capable of infecting people with several curious maladies. On the other hand, opuntias, freely applied, would heal broken bones. What more than likely happened was that while you sat immobilized, picking glochids out of your skin, the fracture had time to heal.

Ancient societies often doctored themselves with locally grown succulents: euphorbia to cure dysentary; sliced Organ-Pipe cactus to remedy diabetes, cancer and ulcers; the juice of *Selenicereus grandiflorus* for the treatment of heart disorders (scientists are still playing around with that one). For cramps? The alkaloids contained in some cereus and mammillarias. No, they didn't cure cramps, they gave them to you.

The old line "How about coming up to see my etchings?" was originally spoken by a Hohokam Indian. Until a few years ago, European armorers were given credit for inventing the etching process in the mid-1400's; then it was discovered that the Hohokams had been etching seashells for centuries before. These shells (pitch coated except for the design) were dunked into an acid bath made of the fermented juice of Saguaro cactus fruit.

COVERT International succulent smugglers? It was going on in 1968, and possibly still is. (I lost track of my "connection" some time ago, so I don't know what the current situation is.)

Growing on both sides of the Rio Grande, in the Big Bend area, there is a slender, dark green succulent which looks like Simonized asparagus. This wax job is what caused the illicit trade in Candelilla. The plant is coated with wax to conserve moisture, a wax used in the manufacture of shoe polish, chewing gum, floor wax and numerous other items.

For a while, Candelilla merchants in Mexico harvested their crop and sold it wherever they could get the best price. The best price was obtainable across the river, in the United States. The Mexican government saw the value of the plant and before anybody could slice off another stalk a marketing monopoly was formed; only the federally owned National Foreign Trade Bank could issue permits to gather Candelilla. Unfortunately, the best price was still to be had across the river. That's when the smuggling began.

As it was easier to sneak out the finished product, "stills" were set up in the woods where the plants were boiled in water and sulphuric acid before the wax was skimmed off. In the finest "revenoor" tradition, these camps were regularly raided by the Feds. On our side of the Rio, the rangers at Big Bend Park are not altogether patient with those who would pilfer the plants growing in the park area.

As much as I hate to put anyone out of work, I think I'll give up polishing my shoes and save a Candelilla.

PEYOTE DECODED As the top of the peyote cactus is the easiest part to get at, and the most loaded with alkaloids, it is usually removed and dried for future use. This dry disk is called a button, and sometimes erroneously called mescal. Mescaline is the primary alkaloid derived from the peyote cactus; mescal is a drink made from a species of agave. Mescal, however, is also an Indian word for fungus, and the dried peyote buttons do look like mushroom tops. You can see how things easily get out of hand.

There are also, traditionally, about 20 plants known in Mexico as peyote. Many of these plants are not even cactus, and while some of them have mind-bending properties, others do not. It is the alkaloids that give peyote these unique properties, and though the top contains the greatest concentration of them, more than 30 alkaloids have been identified throughout the rest of the plant. Alkaloids are organic compounds found in living plants and they contain some of the most powerful medicines and poisons to act upon the human nervous system this side of Lucretia Borgia. They can be both good and bad, depending on the type and the dosage, and they can also be produced synthetically. Besides the alkaloid mescaline, others are caffeine from coffee beans, nicotine from tobacco leaves, quinine from cinchona bark, codeine, morphine and opium from poppy pods, cocaine from cocoa leaves, and atropine and strychnine from nightshade plants.

Federal attempts to control peyote started around 1908, but due to a hodgepodge of regulations the project was abandoned by 1937. From 1937 to 1965, controls were in the hands of the states; then for the next five years the issue was confused by various definitions of the word peyote. Peyote is now defined as "meaning all parts of the plant presently classified as *Lophophora Williamsii Lemaire*, whether growing or not; the seeds thereof; any extract from any part of such plant; and every compound, manufacture, salt, derivative, mixture or preparation of such plant, its seeds or extracts." I think that covers everything!

To legally possess any of the above, a person must first be registered with the Drug Enforcement Administration. Registering, however, is more complex than it sounds. An applicant must meet certain stringent requirements, which sound far above my capabilities. With this news, I have decided to end my illicit cactus growing career before it has begun.

24

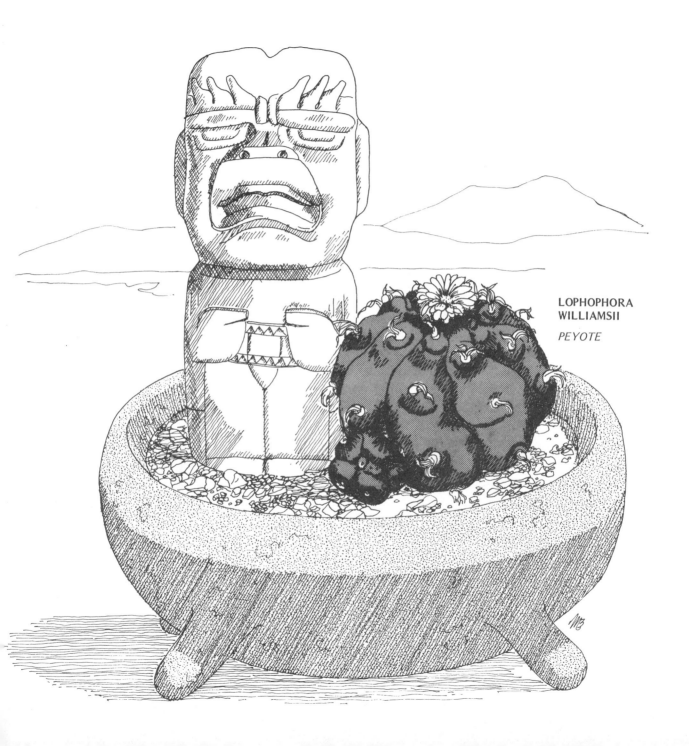

LOPHOPHORA
WILLIAMSII

PEYOTE

the name of the game is botany

THE WAY IT IS FOR ME

First things first, and something I'd like to get over with as soon as possible is the plural term for cactus. To be botanically correct, I suppose it's still cacti. *Webster's New Twentieth Century Dictionary* listing the plurals in order of preference, however, says cactuses first, then cacti. The *American Heritage Dictionary* says vice-versa. It seems you can't talk about more than one cactus without getting into a hassle with somebody. The only solution is to either grow only one cactus or ignore the raised eyebrows when you speak in the plural.

I tried cactuses for a while, but every time I said it I was in front of people who had strong negative feelings about the word. They would stare at me like I had just strangled my grandmother, or had ordered red wine with the fish course, then they would patiently correct me. "It's cacti," they would say. After that happened a few times I got so nervous that I kept forgetting when to stop adding *es's* to cactuses, and I'd end up sounding like a snake with a speech impediment. That didn't suit anybody either, especially at close range.

I switched to cacti. Saying it made me feel very correct, and formal, and intelligent. I knew I wouldn't be able to fake an image like that for very long. Sure enough, within a week's time several of my friends spoke up. "How come you are giving us the 'cacti' bit, when otherwise you are such a clod?" I was going to have to find another word. But what was left? I finally solved the problem by settling on a word which could be argued about by cacti-people and cactuses-people alike. I didn't want anyone to feel left out.

The word is *cactus!* Singular and plural, one or a hundred. Cactus, an all-purpose word, like deer. I find it handy and, strangely enough, very few people are mortally offended by it.

My use of the word cactus is strictly a personal choice, and I suggest you make your own decision, too. Use whatever plural form you are comfortable with and let everyone else have the same privilege. We all have more important things to do than stand around haggling about half of a word! It is another one of those cases where you can either be scientifically and botanically correct, or speak in terms of common usage and plain dirt gardening.

SUCCULENT/CACTUS NOMENCLATURE: AN INTELLECTUAL DISCUSSION
There are some topical terms less controversial than cactus/cacti/cactuses, and I think we should run through them once. Some of you, who are not newcomers, may already know these terms backwards, forwards and sideways, so rather than have you sit there and yawn, why don't you go fix yourself a nice cup of tea? We will be on page 30 when you get back.

Perhaps I should explain that this is not a formal glossary. It is just a few words you won't run into very often if you're not in the plant growing business and a couple of them won't even show up unless you happen to be growing cactus. Besides, everybody knows that if it were a real glossary, it would be in the back of the book. By putting it in the front, it saves a lot of page flipping, not to mention losing your place. There is also no use in prolonging the agony.

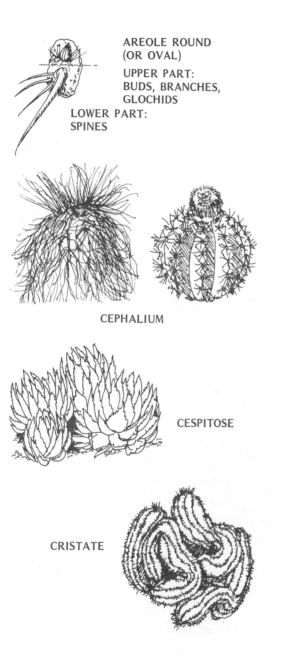

AREOLE ROUND
(OR OVAL)

UPPER PART:
BUDS, BRANCHES,
GLOCHIDS

LOWER PART:
SPINES

CEPHALIUM

CESPITOSE

CRISTATE

GLOSSARY

Areoles These are possessed only by true cactus. They produce spines, flowers, fruits and glochids, and usually look like little felt spots. Yes, they are on the epiphytes, even though they are not as noticeable as they are on desert-type cactus.

Cephalium The woolly cap on the top of certain cactus of flowering size. It contains densely packed areoles which produce bristles and wool, but not spines. The cephalium increases in size each year. There is also a pseudocephalium, which is the hairy growth normal areoles produce: fake fuzz.

Cespitose (or caespitose) If a plant is described as such, it grows in clumps. You'll find this word in many cactus books, but not in this one; if the cactus has a clustering nature, I say so—in those words.

Cristate Crested; used to describe the comblike growth caused by a cactus going totally berserk.

Diurnal Any sensible plant which flowers during the day, as opposed to nocturnal, or night-flowering, is described as diurnal. Plants that insist on blooming in the middle of the night have to come on like gangbusters to be noticed, and become pollinated. Their flowers are most always white, big and white, so they stand out in the darkness. And scented. Insomniac insects need all the directional help they can get, so nocturnal bloomers usually exude a sweet perfume which is about as subtle as a cavalry charge.

Etiolate To become pale, to whiten or blanch; the strung-out growth caused by too little light.

Fasciate Another case of abnormal growth; describes a flattened stem, grossly enlarged. Both types of abnormalities are considered collectors' items and can be quite expensive to buy if they are of any size at all. They are usually grafted onto a normal root stock for preservation, and in the hope that the original maladjusted plant will go crazy and do it again.

Glochids The real troublemakers. They are minute, irritating, crescent-shaped and barbed. Some cactus don't bother with them; others, like the opuntias, make a fetish out of them and then they are notoriously lethal. The only certain method of removing them from your person is to rent an electron microscope and an accompanying steady-handed technician.

Offsets Little plants which grow at the base of the parent plant, usually occurring in the clumping kinds of cactus and other succulents. They are very easy to break off and root for propagation purposes.

Tubercles The tubers or lumps, sometimes called "chins," on some types of cactus. Others have vertical ribs, and some are as smooth as a baby's bottom.

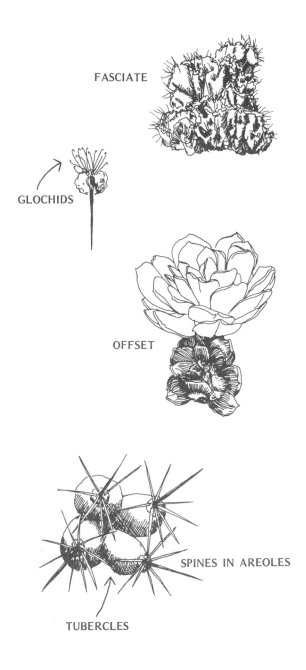

FASCIATE

GLOCHIDS

OFFSET

SPINES IN AREOLES

TUBERCLES

IT'S ALL GREEK TO ME

Prospective cactus/succulent owners are often put off by the formidable names which seem to plague these plants. They have a point.

Taxonomy is the section of botany dealing with the names and classifications of plants. People who decide on the names and persist on reshuffling classifications are called taxonomists, although there have been occasions when I have called them names I felt were eminently more suitable.

The father of taxonomy, and of modern botany, was a man called Linnaeus, Carolus Linnaeus. The name conjures up visions of an ancient sage, somebody who played ball with Cicero. The vision is deceiving. He lived in the mid-18th century and he was Swedish—Carl von Linne. He is always referred to in the Latinized version, and even used it himself in his later years. Shows you how far botanists will go to keep things pure.

Linnaeus was the one who started the system of using two Latin names to identify plants—one for genus and one for species. Before that, plants were scientifically known by phrases a half dozen, or more, words long. Thinking the old system was needlessly wordy, he set out to simplify the situation. Whether he did or not is still a matter for speculation.

One of the first things he did was to shorten melocactus to cactus. It was one of the few words he ever shortened. The old *phrases* got shorter, but the *words* got longer.

Linnaeus may have recognized a goodly number of other plants, but he only knew some 20-odd cactus plants, and he called them all "cactus." This, as we shall see, got everybody into a lot of trouble later on.

When we sprain our eyeballs on triple-jointed botanical names, we wonder why on earth old Carl decided to use Latin. What's wrong with Swedish? Or English? The language of all sciences, I am told, is Latin because it is a dead language and therefore static and unchanging. If it was *anthos* (flower) in ancient Rome, it's still *anthos* today. Of course, Greek and Latin sort of ran together for a time, so what hasn't been "Latinized" has been "Greeked." Then you can throw in a little Old German, and there you have it. A scientific language.

Botanical names are made up of two or three descriptive Latin, Greek or whatever, words combined to form a single word, and as the classification system demands two such compound words (three, if you include variety) for each plant, you can see we are in trouble already. Something like *Echinofossulocactus pentacanthus* is bound to pop up sooner or later. Translation:

echinos (hedgehog, sometimes sea urchin)
fossula (grooved)
penta (five)
canthus (a spine, from *akanthos*)

So what we have here is a prickly, grooved or ribbed cactus with five spines per areole. A while back this cactus had an easier name: *Stenocactus*, *steno* meaning narrow and referring to the most obvious characteristic . . . thin, prominent ribs.

Taxonomists switch generic names on us with great regularity. Species names are changed more often than your socks. Some cactus are listed and sold under more than one name, and some have a trail of synonyms behind them as long as your arm. The notation "name under which species was previously known" is fairly common in cactus catalogs. It gets to the point where we want to leap up

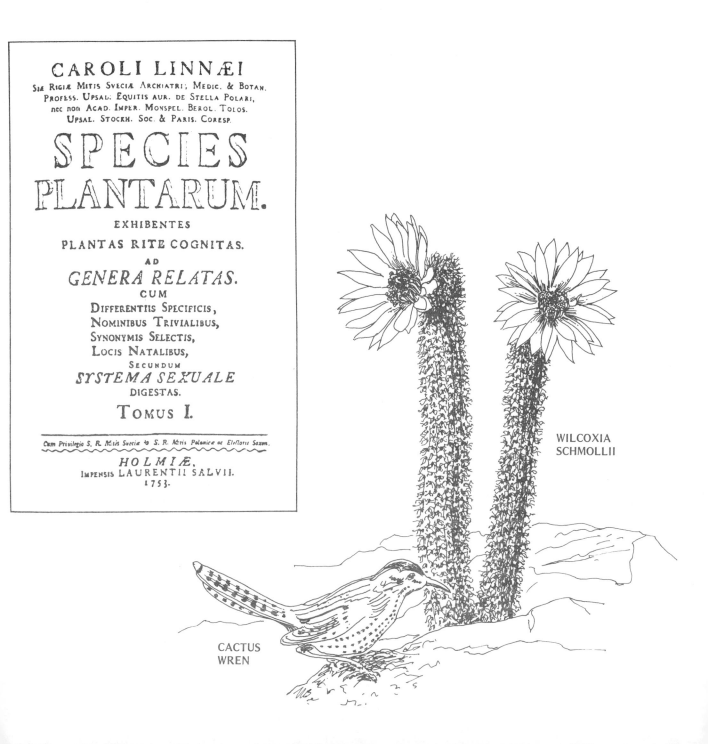

CAROLI LINNÆI

Sæ Regiæ Mtis Sveciæ Archiatri; Medic. & Botan.
Profess. Upsal: Equitis aur. de Stella Polari,
nec non Acad. Imper. Monspel. Berol. Tolos.
Upsal. Stockh. Soc. & Paris. Coresp.

SPECIES PLANTARUM.

EXHIBENTES

PLANTAS RITE COGNITAS.

AD

GENERA RELATAS.

CUM

DIFFERENTIIS SPECIFICIS,
NOMINIBUS TRIVIALIBUS,
SYNONYMIS SELECTIS,
LOCIS NATALIBUS,
SECUNDUM
SYSTEMA SEXUALE
DIGESTAS.

TOMUS I.

Cum Privilegio S. R. Mtis Sveciæ & S. R. Mtis Polonicæ ac Electoris Saxon.

HOLMIÆ,
IMPENSIS LAURENTII SALVII.
1753.

WILCOXIA
SCHMOLLII

CACTUS
WREN

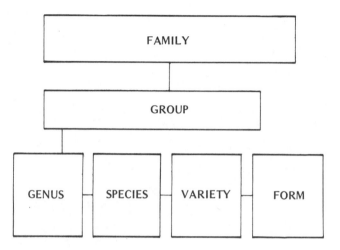

```
              ┌─────────────────────────────────────┐
              │               FAMILY                │
              └─────────────────────────────────────┘
                                │
                   ┌────────────────────────┐
                   │          GROUP          │
                   └────────────────────────┘
                       │
        ┌────────┐  ┌────────┐  ┌────────┐  ┌────────┐
        │ GENUS  │──│SPECIES │──│VARIETY │──│  FORM  │
        └────────┘  └────────┘  └────────┘  └────────┘
```

and yell, "Who cares?" It is quite obvious that somebody does; we will have to put up with it.

According to some authorities, many genera and species of plants are blessed, or cursed, with a sub-something. According to others, there aren't any sub-anythings! Whether there are such things or not depends on how picky each botanist wants to get. For instance: Should the *Cephalocereus* growing in South America be called by the same name as the *Cephalocereus* growing in Mexico? Is it a completely different genus? Or is it the same genus regardless of location? Or should it be called a sub-genus?

Some of the botanical names used in this book, and other books, may be dubbed a sub- by somebody somewhere, and except for the terribly serious-minded student of botany, I don't think anybody really cares too much.

Very often one of the botanical names will be the Latinized version of a man's surname, and they usually end in *ii* or *i; Marsoneri, Parkinsonii, Armstrongii.* These honorees are most likely the discoverers of the species, although hybridizers, buyers, sellers, collectors and some who are just good friends also get into the act.

Speaking of names, whoever thought up *Mesembryanthemum* should have been taken out and shot! (It was probably a spare-time stockbroker who had cornered the eraser market.) To avoid strangulation these little South African succulents are commonly called mesembs: *mesos,* middle; *embryon,* fruit; *anthemon,* flower. Put them all together and they spell pebble plants, or split rocks. These are succulents which fruit and flower right in the middle, between the two halves of the plant, which can be anywhere from two distinct sections to a small slit on the top of one basic "pebble."

A FEW TRANSLATIONS

I'm sure you've noticed by now that if you happen to have been born with a silver dictionary in your mouth, you can break those long word combinations down and get a pretty good idea of what a plant looks like, or what its outstanding characteristic is, or where it comes from. Some day when you are a couple of bucks to the good, buy a botanical dictionary. They are not amusing, but they are interesting.

There are some Latin words that show up regularly in the cactus world, and even when they are combined with other words they are recognizable and helpful; especially if you are ordering out of a catalog lacking in color fold-outs.

For example, *senilis* turns up as a species name in many genera. This one is not hard to figure. It means old, senile and white haired, and is most always applied to cactus with long, white hair. Sometimes it refers to white spines, but only when the spines are long and dense enough to look like the real thing. *Senilis* is an apt and picturesque name, although I do take exception to the implication that anyone with white hair is an idiot.

I once thought I had a rare gray-haired species. Then I discovered the source of the hair. My Persian cat kept brushing past the cactus on his way to a sunny siesta in the window. I should have known. The cat looked exceptionally well groomed and the cactus only had hair on one side.

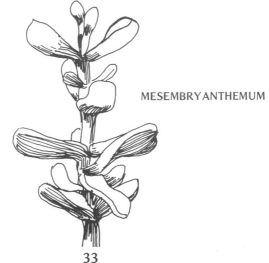

MESEMBRYANTHEMUM

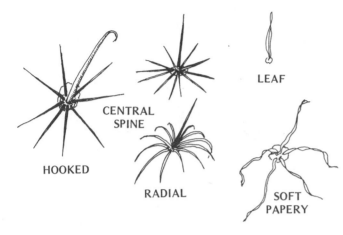

HOOKED

CENTRAL SPINE

LEAF

RADIAL

SOFT PAPERY

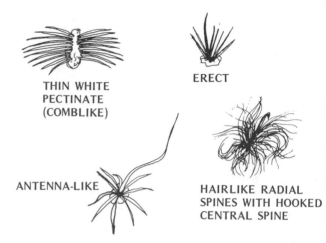

THIN WHITE PECTINATE (COMBLIKE)

ERECT

ANTENNA-LIKE

HAIRLIKE RADIAL SPINES WITH HOOKED CENTRAL SPINE

HOW TO BE PUNCTURED: IN GREEK

Spines come in a wide assortment of shapes, sizes and colors, and their description is very often a part of a botanical name. There are two "spine" words: *spina* and *acantho* or *acanthus*. They are combined with other words, as in:

albispina white spines.

aureispina golden spines.

brevispina short, mercifully brief spines.

dasyacanthus covered with soft spines (*dasys:* hairy in the fuzzy form).

leucacanthus white spines.

phyllacantha flat, leaf-like spines (*phyllos:* leaf).

polycanthus many spines.

pubispina small soft spines, as if they are permanently going through puberty.

Other spine prefixes include *micro* (small), *macro* (large) and *densi* (dense). Even more horrifying is *mega!* The Greek word for toothed is *odous,* so we can add *acanthodes* (toothed spines) to the list.

As hedgehogs and sea urchins are pretty prickly individuals, taxonomists thought the word *echino*

(either hedgehog or sea urchin, in botany the two are interchangeable) was a handy thing to have around. So *Echinofossulocactus, Echinopsis, Echinocactus* and *Echinocereus* were foisted off on us.

Wait a minute! How come there is an *Echino*cactus and an *Echino*cereus? They are both cactus plants, aren't they? Of course they are. The cactus/cereus thing is the result of botanists trying to get themselves out of a pit into which they had inadvertently fallen. It started a long time ago and part of the blame must fall onto the shoulders of that Swedish-Latin, Linnaeus.

The first cactus to make it to Europe alive, way back when, was a round melon-shaped number: melocactus they called it. Shortly after, more cactus plants survived the trip and they too were classified as melocactus, even though they weren't necessarily that shape. Linnaeus shortened the word to cactus, hoping to get out of the melon business and the image it projected, but he clearly did not know what he had let himself in for. There were many, many more kinds of cactus than he, or anyone else, had imagined there would be.

When the tall, columnar cactus began showing up, the botanical people decided it was a little ridiculous to call them by a name that had been inspired by a cantaloupe, so they called these tall cactus cereus (waxy or torchlike).

Consequently, *Echinocactus* is a short sea urchin, and *Echinocereus* is a tall hedgehog, or is it a short hedgehog and a tall sea urchin? Generally speaking, the term cactus when used as part of the generic name still means globular, and cereus means columnar, whether erect or sprawling like temple ruins. You can get into a lot of trouble, however, when you speak "generally" about the cactus family, because there is always some fool exception, as Linnaeus found out. *Zygocactus,* an epiphyte, is certainly not globe shaped, but if you apply the cactus/cereus theory to only desert types, you'll be in good shape.

FLORAL AND FRUIT CLUES

Botanical names often include some bit of information about flowers, and if you know what to look for it can be helpful if the specimen you are interested in is not blooming at the time. The two "flower" words to watch for are *flora* and *anthos.* The color of the flower is often sneaked into the species name.

alba white in variations; *albescens, albiflora,* etc.

aureis golden.

boscasana yellow.

rubescens red, but not gory.

sanguiniflora bloody red.

ECHINOCACTUS
HORIZONTHALONIUS

ECHINOCEREUS
DELAETII

Other than color, the flowers may be described by the term:

arachnacantha cobwebby (arachnoid).

If you think you have some of these, check to be sure by dusting oftener.

Then, by adding *anthos* or *flora* you can run through the whole *micro/macro* business again. Plus: *grandi*, *multi* and *magni*.

Some words refer to the position of the flower: *secundiflora* means side flowering; *corypantha (koryphe:* summit or top) means the flowers appear smack on top of the plant. *Terminalis* (on the ends) is when flowers are on the very ends of stems or branches, or if the flowers themselves are *fimbriata* (fringed) *terminalis*, they would be fringed on the ends. Naturally, in the case of the well-known *Coryfimbriata Surryii*, it would be "The Surrey with the Fringe on the Top."

If the fruit is mentioned, *karpos* is the word, although it usually turns up in the *capra* or *carpus* form.

acanthocarpa spiny fruit.

ariocarpus resembles the fruit of the white beam tree *(aria)*.

encephalocarpus head-shaped fruit.

turbinicarpus top-shaped fruit.

Yes, indeed, *micro-(carpa)* and *macro-(carpa)* are still with us.

Sometimes *phytos* or *phytum* (plant) is used in one of the botanical names, as in *Astrophytum* (Star plant). Fortunately, there are also quite a few botanical names that are self-explanatory and easy to translate: *horrida, variegata, elegans, columnaris, compactum, prostratus, pendula, elongata, globuse,* to name some.

IT'S ONE OF THOSE, AGAIN

There are two words you will see time and time again—*opsis* and *pseudo. Opsis* (like or resembling) is suffixed onto many plant names.

Echinopsis like a hedgehog.

Mamillopsis nipple-like, or resembling a mammillaria cactus.

Pereskiopsis like the *Pereskia* cactus.

And as *Rhipsalis* means wickerwork, you can safely conclude that *Rhipsalidopsis* means looks like wickerwork, leading us to believe that both of these plants resemble porch furniture.

Pseudo (false or fake) used as a prefix, is tacked onto more botanical names than anyone cares to think about. It was an escape route for all the times a plant was classified as one thing and then later turned out to be something else. *Opsis* and *pseudo* saved the day for taxonomists more than once. Sometimes they got a little carried away with themselves, and the *pseudo/opsis* lunacy culminated when *Pseudoechinopsis* was put together. *Echinopsis*, resembling a hedgehog, I'll buy. But *Pseudoechinopsis?* Resembling a fake hedgehog?

After that one, there is absolutely nothing more to be said on the subject of botanical names, except don't worry about them. We are not growing names, we are growing plants. If you can't remember the botanical handle of a cactus two minutes after you get it out of the store, just take it home and call it Fred. It won't care a whit.

There is also a certain satisfaction to be had by looking right into the eyes of anyone who asks about a plant, and saying, "I haven't the faintest idea what it is." Chances are one in a million that they don't know either, or they wouldn't have asked, and you can feel humble together.

CEPHALOCEREUS

ECHEVERIA

SORTING THEM OUT

There are two kinds of succulents: leaf and stem. Cactus fall into the stem category, as that is exactly what they are—fat stems. The other succulent plants, ranging from those *with* plump leaves to those that *are* plump leaves, are in the leaf class.

Cactus also come in two flavors: desert and jungle. Most of them are of the desert type, but there are quite a few jungle dwellers and they are called epiphytes (air plants). Orchids and bromeliads are epiphytic, too. These plants are not parasites living off a host plant; they simply use trees and logs as a perching place. Evidently they just like the view. They also want to get a little more light and as they are not true climbers, having no grasping tendrils, they must start high in the first place. On the jungle floor the light is quite dim and growing plants are few; the overhead canopy of leaves is usually thick enough to suppress undergrowth. Soil is also apt to be very poor in a rain forest or jungle. There is no wholesale autumn leaf drop: Only a few leaves fall throughout the year, and they decompose very quickly because of the hordes of fungi, insects and bacteria living there.

Humus accumulates only in small amounts and steady rains leach out the minerals. Epiphytes are better off up in the trees where there is more fresh air movement, more light and often more humus.

But if you want to live in the penthouse you have to pay the price, and epiphytes had to forfeit their earthbound roots. The jungle soil may be poor but the supply of moisture is abundant. To move upward they had to develop some of the same moisture-saving devices as the desert cactus, such as waxy coatings and spongy roots.

Epiphytic cactus are usually trailers, semi-climbers or leaners and many of them produce aerial roots to help anchor themselves and also to absorb moisture from the air. They like heat and humidity, partial shade, an acid humusy soil and warmish winters. (There is no real winter in the jungle, just a wet and a dry season. The so-called dry season is only *dry* by comparison.) Because of these preferences the culture for epiphytes is different than it is for desert cactus and it is best that their care and feeding be investigated in a section of their own.

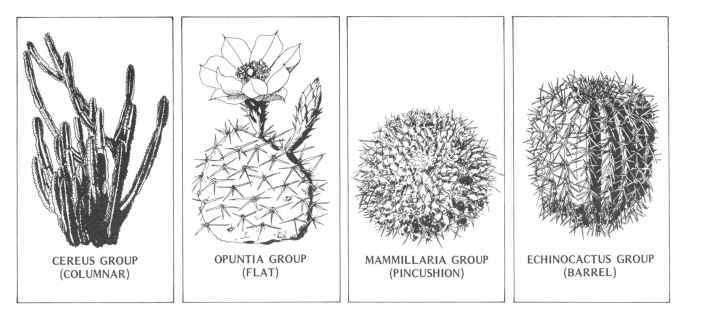

| CEREUS GROUP (COLUMNAR) | OPUNTIA GROUP (FLAT) | MAMMILLARIA GROUP (PINCUSHION) | ECHINOCACTUS GROUP (BARREL) |

DESERT CACTUS, LOOSELY SPEAKING

Desert cactus can be divided into four categories or groups.

- Obvious stems, either erect (Organ-Pipe) or prostrate (Peanut cactus); these are the cereus types.
- Large, barrel shaped or cylindrical (Barrel cactus), which includes the echinocactus and friends.
- Small, low-growing plants that grow singly or in clusters (mammillarias or pincushion types).
- Flat pads or sausage-like joints growing out of each other (the opuntias).

These four divisions are, of course, only spoken of in general terms, as there is always the exception. You have no idea how many serious botanists will go out and hurl themselves off a cliff over generalities like these. The botanical term group is used as a general division denoting description, based on a plant's most obvious physical characteristic. Usually this can be decided by viewing the plant from some 20 feet away: Does it look like a barrel or a pincushion? Does it have pads and joints or is it a continuous stem? You may not know if that cactus in the distance is a *Pilosocereus*, a *Cephalocereus*, a *Lemaireocereus* or a *Echinocereus*, but you will at least know that it is *some kind* of cereus. Or if a grower says "I collect only the pincushion types," he or she may have 20 genera of cactus, but they will all be little, clustering, round plants. You can bet on it.

Though some cactus authorities divide the desert cactus into several more groups than are given here, these divisions will suffice for the purposes of this book.

THERE MUST BE ANOTHER WAY!

Some succulent books arrange plants alphabetically, some group them according to country of origin, and some divide them into botanical groups. My divisions are made on size, shape and temperament. Why? Well, suppose . . .

Somewhere, sometime, you saw a little, round white cactus that looked like a fuzzy golf ball, but you didn't get the name of it and nobody down at the corner poolhall knew what it was either. When you asked the local nursery owner, he said you had finally flipped your lid. So, what's left? You visit the library and look through a cactus book—and look, and look. No picture that even comes close. Nothing listed under *Golfballia fuzzii* in the index; just pages and pages of strange, unpronounceable names. In desperation, you begin on page one and keep going, and after reading 952 species descriptions, all of which turn out to be neither round, small nor white, you consider giving it up. About that time some quaint individual adds to your misery by asking if you are sure it is really a cactus—and you do give up. (People have been led down the cactus path by other succulents that are magnificent imposters.)

By making divisions based on physical characteristics, I hope to save you some time in hunting for your particular lost plant. You may find out it isn't in this book either, but it won't take as long.

Of course, with a system like this, it's possible for different species of one genus to show up in more than one category. For instance, mammillarias with white hair in one section; mammillarias without in another. In a situation like this, detailed natural history, political affiliation and church preference will be found where a genus' appearance is most fully explored. When the genus is grouped with others as an example of a physical characteristic, generic information is reduced to name, rank and serial number, although species peculiarities will be included in both places. For your convenience, generic duplications, if any, have been noted.

This may sound confusing, but I still think it's easier for the beginning succulent fan to recognize a shape or physical feature rather than a long-winded name.

AUTHOR'S NOTE

One thing, before we get on with it. To verbally describe a plant it is necessary to mention the color of it, and what one person calls grayish green, another may call greenish gray. Colors actually may differ for the same plant, depending on the location, soil type and variation in the species. You also have to make allowances for the describer's eye for color. Anyway, don't be alarmed if I say a certain cactus is blue-green and your friend on the table looks plain green to you. It probably is.

All species listed from here on out respond well to general cactus/succulent culture, unless otherwise mentioned. If you don't have the faintest idea what "general culture" is, it will be explored later.

II INDOOR PLANTS

REBUTIA

the well adjusted

The succulents in this section know how to behave and are docile, even though some of them have quite an array of spines. Most of them are small or medium sized. Some will eventually get big, but not back-you-into-a-corner *big*. No plant in this group will give you nervous prostration, frighten your children, or severely test your green thumb; they are only slightly more ominous than the yellow pages.

A few of the South African succulents may seem to have mental problems because they try very hard to look like cactus, but they really are quite well adjusted and just like to pretend. Humor them along and they'll be fine.

These plants need no further introduction, except to say that they have been divided into three groups: globular, small to medium; columnar; and bushy and hanging.

the well adjusted: globular

REBUTIA

All right, you think you'd like to try growing a cactus, but you never have had one and you're not sure how to take care of it. What you want is something easy, something to experiment with and keep you company while you're reading.

Trot off to the nearest nursery and look for a plant tagged *Rebutia*. Any species or variety will do. They are usually easy to find and quite inexpensive. They are also small and quick to bloom, and it takes a direct hit with an atomic bomb to kill a rebutia. If the soil is completely dry when you get it home, water it; if the soil is damp, leave it alone. Set it on a sunny windowsill and don't fuss about not knowing what to do next. Rebutias are perfectly willing to wait around until you find out. It won't be long anyway.

Rebutias, named for P. Rebut, a French collector and dealer, are small, clustering, spiny, globe-shaped plants with low tubercles arranged in spirals. Their natural home is in the mountains of Argentina and Bolivia, between the 4,000- to 16,000-foot levels. Because the sun at these altitudes and latitudes is very intense—abetted by smog-free air—they grow among wild grasses, which offer some protection from the strong rays of summer and also a little insulation in the winter. The rest of the time they just sit there, half hidden, waiting to give some soft-lipped grazing animal the shock of a lifetime.

Rebutias were discovered during the time of the last big cactus rage, between World Wars I and II. It probably happened when some tired botanist flung himself down to take a nap on what he thought was a comfortable mountain meadow. Rebutias immediately became popular with the windowsill set: The plants stayed small, were very hardy and were easily propagated from offsets. Their popularity was greatly aided by the fact that they bloomed at a very early age, some when only an inch high. There were several kinds to choose from, although they all had flowers in varying shades of red.

Then, in 1935, a golden-yellow flowering species was discovered *(R. Marsoneri)* and rebutia collectors went wild. It may not seem like so much now, but at the time it was the greatest thing that had happened to the cactus world since the invention of the tweezers. Since then, with more discoveries and because they hybridize easily, rebutias have expanded further into the color spectrum. They are now available in many shades of red, orange, pink, yellow, violet and white.

The flowers are of the typical cactus type—funnel-shaped. They rise from old areoles at the base of the plant and are very abundant, often more flowers than plant. Like most other cactus flowers, they do not last long, but as there are lots of them you can be assured of continuous bloom over a fairly long period of time.

Some growers think the plant itself is relatively short-lived, but even if it does go out in a frenzy of bloom after a few years, there are usually plenty of offsets by then to take the place of the deceased parent plant. Older plants get gray around the base; it's the nature of the beast and is not disfiguring, or a sign that something has gone haywire.

Many species are so closely related that they are treated as varieties by some botanists and growers. Until the argument is settled, which may be never, I will list them under the aliases I last saw them using. *R. grandiflora*, for instance, may be tagged as either a variety of *R. miniscula* or as a separate species. No matter, it's still the same lovely little creature.

R. albiflora A very small plant, often grafted onto another root stock. White spines and flowers.

R. calliantha This one is larger and more cylindrical than the others. Up to six inches high, with white spines and very large red flowers.

R. grandiflora Large red flowers with long tubes. Tops of flowers higher than the plant.

R. Marsoneri A very small, light green plant with white spines and big golden-yellow flowers. Don't panic! The buds are supposed to be reddish brown.

R. miniscula (Red-Crown) A bright green plant with short whitish spines and many red flowers in the spring. Especially hardy as a house plant.

R. muscula Light orangy flowers and many soft white spines.

R. pulvinosa A short cylinder with fine spines. The flowers are small and orange.

R. senilis (Fire-Crown) A dark green plant with thick, long white spines; very bright red flowers.

R. violaciflora Ginger-brown spines and rosy-violet flowers that may appear in late winter instead of spring. It may be listed as a variety of *R. miniscula*.

R. xanthocarpa Short white spines and small red flowers. The *salmonea* form has salmon-pink flowers.

POT CULTURE Rebutias expect to be dry and cool in the winter, as they were raised in the mountains. In the spring while the buds are forming they should be watered frequently enough to keep the soil from going bone dry. In their natural setting these cactus, and others from high altitudes, collect a considerable amount of moisture from the morning dew, so if you are misting some of your other plants you can give it a squirt once in awhile, instead of a regular watering.

After blooming, rebutias take a short rest. It's exhausting for such a tiny plant to put out as many flowers as it does—a two incher can produce dozens—and it needs a little time to regroup before it gets on with the business at hand. Don't mistake this resting period for an indication that you have done something wrong. It will start growing again as soon as it gets ready.

If you live where it gets blisteringly hot in the summer, give this cactus a spot where it will get full morning sun, but filtered sun during the hottest part of the afternoon. Try to make up for the grass it no longer has to snuggle down into.

How much water? In that respect they are like any other plant. The answer depends on so many circumstances that it is impossible to make any definite rule or timetable. Just keep in mind that no cactus likes to be sitting in a potful of dry dust, or a continually damp soil. As I said, rebutias are tough; they will not drop dead.

Rebutias set seed quite freely. In autumn the seedpods will often pop open if they haven't been picked off, and seeds will fall into the pot . . . or the pot of a close neighbor. The seed is dry (no pulp) and it germinates easily. Small offsets are also easily propagated.

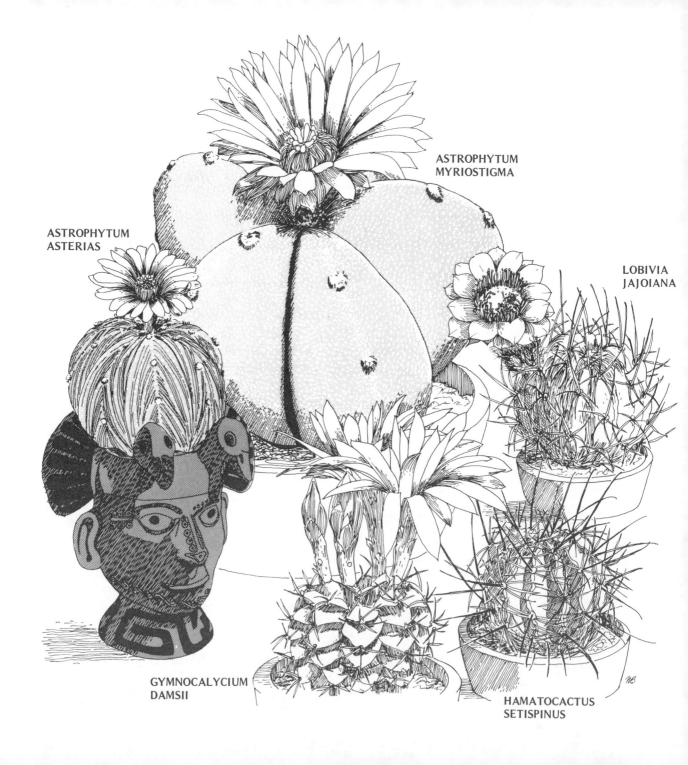

ASTROPHYTUM
MYRIOSTIGMA

ASTROPHYTUM
ASTERIAS

LOBIVIA
JAJOIANA

GYMNOCALYCIUM
DAMSII

HAMATOCACTUS
SETISPINUS

LOBIVIA

On the surface, *Lobivia* are well adjusted: They are small, neat, round plants, their culture is among the easiest of all cactus, and they are very free flowering. They are, however, one third of the scandalous *Chamaecereus, Echinopsis, Lobivia* triangle, a group well known for its loose morals and hybrid children (Johnson 'Paramount' hybrids). The name *Lobivia* itself suggests an exotic dancer —Lobivia and Her Doves—but it is really the result of taxonomists playing around with the name of the country where many of these plants grow: Bolivia.

Argentina and Peru also have their share of these small, usually clustering plants which often have a tuberous, turnip-like taproot. Many of them have strong spines and a few have insulating hair. They grow on the slopes of the Andes, at anywhere from 8,000 to 15,000 feet, enduring winter temperatures as cold as 5° F. In preparation for the chilling, they start the winter in a very dry condition to prevent freezing, with only a little moisture stored underground in the thick root. They also tend to hide by embedding themselves deeply in the soil, or crouching under other plants, or snuggling down between a couple of rocks.

Their flowers are funnel shaped, large (to four inches across) and brilliantly colored; red, purple, orange, yellow, pink and white. They are bright and profuse, and alas, short-lived—only one day when the weather is hot. But, as the buds do not open all at the same time, they still make quite a display.

Lobivias were once listed under the genus *Echinopsis,* and possibly should have been left there. The classification of plants in both genera has been difficult. Has been? No! It still is. When I researched these two cactus, I ended up with 11 pages of confused notes and a terrible sinking feeling. Each expert I consulted had a different opinion! Some said there were not only *Lobivia* and *Echinopsis,* but *Pseudolobivia* and *Pseudoechinopsis* as well; others said that the whole thing was a figment of somebody's imagination. There is even some disagreement over whether the hybrids are *Echinobivia* or *Lobiviopsis.*

A single plant can be listed under three or four different names, depending on who is doing the name calling. When I went through my notes and weeded out the duplications, 11 pages dwindled to five. I did some name calling of my own!

The following list of species will be brief . . . and totally unreliable. Besides the man-made befuddlement, there seems to be a great deal of natural variation within each individual species.

L. aurea A small cactus, about four inches both ways when mature, bearing splendid, glowing yellow flowers on a short hairy stem. Ribs covered with light-colored radial spines; one dark central spine sticks straight up, so watch it!

L. Jajoiana About the same size as the *aurea,* with dark green ribs divided into tubercles. Radial spines with darker centrals, and one long hooked spine. Flowers two to three inches across; deep red with purplish-black throat.

As far as I can determine, other red flowering species include *L. cinnabarina, L. Hertrichiana, L. Higginsiana, L. Pentlandii* and *L. planiceps. L. leucomalla* has white flowers and *L. kermesina* (a lighter green plant than the others with needle-sharp spines) has reddish-pink bloom.

Not much to go on, I must admit. In regard to the many other beautifully flowered species, the experts agree on only one thing: The plants are all cactus! Don't let that stop you from trying any lobivia who happens to show up on your doorstep. There isn't a one of them who will disappoint you, even if you haven't been properly introduced.

POT CULTURE Very easy; the only cactus less demanding is *Echinopsis,* which follows. Lobivias with large taproots should have a bigger pot; otherwise give them the usual cactus treatment. Good for beginners; a mistake here and there will do them no harm.

Propagate by offsets or cuttings. Seed germinates easily.

ECHINOPSIS

The South American hedgehog *(echino)* like *(opsis)* consort of the *Lobivia.* Rich green, round, spiny plants with beautiful nocturnal flowers. In their natural habitat they grow in fairly rich soil and enjoy a damper climate than many other cactus. As house plants they will adapt to many conditions. They are among the least particular about soil, sun and water.

Many people, who are already interested in the echinopsis because of the easy culture aspect, come completely unglued when they read about the flowers. "Ten-inch bloom" sounds too good to be true! And if you get right down to brass tacks, it isn't exactly true. The flowers are large, to be sure, but they are also on the end of a hairy, spiny stem and the stem is included in that 10-inch measurement. Isn't that cheating? Not really. This type of stem growth is technically part of the flower.

There is good reason for the flower to be so tall. Echinopsis don't usually grow in the middle of 40 acres of open ground. They live where the landscape is often rough, surrounded by other kinds of vegetation. As small cactus, echinopsis appreciate the protection of taller plants, but as night bloomers they also had better get their flowers "up there" where they can be seen. Pollinating insects like white flowers and they like sweet flowers; they do not like a treasure hunt. A long-stemmed flower was the only answer.

Echinopsis are hardy, rapid growers and they produce offsets freely. For best flowering, remove the offsets and pot up separately; a plant three inches across is mature enough to bloom.

E. aurea Less round than many of the others and about four inches high. Produces many offsets and exceptional yellow flowers.

E. Eyriesii (Easter Lily Cactus) A globe when young, columnar with age. Dark green with prominent ribs bearing large whitish areoles and short, stiff spines. White, sweet-scented flowers are large and lovely. This parent has many varieties.

E. kermesina Round and spiny. Flowers look like red lilies.

E. multiplex Large rose-pink flowers, trumpet-shaped and sweet. The plant is dark green and globular with long, thick spines. Short-spined plants with pink flowers may be a cross between *multiplex* and *Eyriesii;* sometimes correctly labeled as such, other times not.

E. turbinata Top-shaped with large, sweet, white flowers.

POT CULTURE If their culture was any easier it would be embarrassing! Full sun or part shade in summer. High temperatures and hours of hot sun are not necessary for good culture. Can be fertilized during growing and blooming periods when they are quite active for members of the cactus family.

Propagation by offsets, which are usually numerous, or from seed.

Although by nature echinopsis are nocturnally flowering, I've heard you can fake them out by shutting them in a closet for a half hour or so.

WITH A CAST OF THOUSANDS

Lobivia-Echinopsis hybrids produce lovely flowers; large, like the echinopsis, and brilliantly colored, like the lobivia. Many are fragrant. The only problem here is that they have one nocturnally blooming parent (echinopsis) and one diurnal (lobivia). The hybrids lean toward night flowering, but some of them get a bad case of the yawns after opening about halfway, and wait till morning to finish up. The following *Lobiviopsis* hybrids may be listed under either Lobivia or Echinopsis in catalogs.

X 'Aurora' Yellow throated salmon-pink flowers.

X 'Green Gold' Bright yellow flowers. Plant very sharply ribbed, like a pleated paper lantern. Scented.

X 'Peach Monarch' Large, satinlike peach flower.

X 'Red Riding Hood' and X 'Red Paramount' Glowing red flowers on both.

X 'Tangerine' Small, but profuse, orangy flowers.

X 'Terra Cotta' Scented, very large flower; pink with salmon mid-stripe.

X 'Tricolor' Blended flowers of red, white and yellow.

X 'White Knight' A favorite. White flowers up to five inches across.

POT CULTURE Like their parents, the hybrids are easy to care for. Give them the usual cactus treatment. These plants are vigorous growers, although some of them do not readily form offsets. If you want to increase the herd, cut off the top of the plant (it's easy to root); the base will then put out several new sprouts. Seed germinates easily.

GYMNOCALYCIUM

There are nearly 100 species of this small, globular cactus from South America. Although the genus itself has always been very stable, with few changes in membership, there has been a terrible ado about defining the differences between some species and varieties. Many of them have more aliases than a bunco artist.

Their naked *(gymnos)* flower buds *(kalyx)* are their most noticeable characteristic, along with their chinlike tubercles. Spines vary in shape and length; almost every type is represented on one species or another. The flowers are large, about two inches, and long lasting. The blooming period is also lengthy: from spring through summer, often into early fall.

These cactus have always been popular with home growers because of their easy culture and many flowers. Their native climate is damp and mild, and they grow partially shaded, conditions which are compatible with our homes.

In the United States and Japan there has been much hybridizing of the gymnocalycium, with some startling results. The results are often sold under the name Moon cactus—grafted, no-chlorophyll oddities of bright color.

G. Baldianum A slightly flattened globe, blue-gray and about three inches across at maturity. The few spines are short and radial with no centrals. Most gymnocalyciums have white, pink or yellow flowers, so the dark red blooms of this one caused quite a stir back around the turn of the century when it was discovered.

G. Damsii (Dam's Chin cactus) Will grow well from seed, flowers when young and has striped markings. The chins are very pronounced and topped with fine, small bristlelike spines. Flowers are pink or white. There are several variations on the *Damsii* theme—all attractive.

G. Mihanovichii A two-inch plant with many varieties. It has a strong rib and tubercle development (similar to the *Damsii*) and is grayish green with reddish markings and long, curved radial spines. Flowers freely when very small; color varies between pink and yellow.

G. Mihanovichii var. *Friedrichii* The name is bigger than the plant and sounds like a Romanian law firm, but because of all the crazy crossbreeding it is necessary. This combination, plus a little witchcraft, has produced the cultivar 'Ruby Ball,' from Japan, where it's known as 'Hibotan.' It is bright, clear red and looks quite unreal. Another is 'Hibotan Nishiki,' with red and green stripes. White and waxy yellow plants are also quite common. These strange little creatures do not flower readily, often not at all, but with all that color in the body of the plant, who needs flowers? Having not a drop of chlorophyll, they are always grown grafted to a nice green base.

G. Monvillei An attractive cactus with radial spines which are reddish at the base and pale yellow at the tip. Flowers from white to light pink.

POT CULTURE Easy! Does not need long periods in hot sun. During growing and flowering season, see that it has ample water; do not let it stay dry for very long, if you want to keep those flowers coming. Usual winter rest with cooler temperatures.

Propagation is best from seed. From seedling to flowering size is not a long wait; plants will flower when very young.

MAMMILLARIA

For life history, see "Mammillaria" in The Fair-Haired Boys cactus section.

M. camptotricha (Bird's-nest cactus) Clustering, slender stems, with close-set, white, starlike radial spines. Very springy and fun to touch. The white flowers are nothing spectacular, but they give off a sweet, citrus-flower smell.

M. elongata (Golden Stars) Fast growing, dense clumps of erect stems. Each tubercle tipped with many golden spines in a starlike pattern. Creamy flower. *M. fragilis* (or *M. gracilis*), the Thimble cactus, has similar growth but rounder stems of pale green covered with star spines. Because the clusters fall apart very easily, there is no problem acquiring offsets. Flowers are pinkish outside, creamy inside.

M. Sheldonii Cylindrical, grayish-green stems to 10 inches, clustering from the base. Light radial spines with lower, dark central hooked. Large flowers are pink, some with darker pink mid-stripe. Will bloom while very young, but also prone to root rot.

M. Wildii One of the most common. Vigorous and clustering, to about one foot across with many, many heads. A single plant is about four inches high and six across, but you would have to remove offsets like mad to keep a solitary plant. Areoles produce eight or 10 white spines with yellowish centrals; lower one hooked. The ring of flowers on top may bloom through the summer; white with pinkish cast.

M. Zeilmanniana Small, two and a half inches high and two inches wide, densely nippled and dark green. Radial spines are thin and white with four brown centrals; lower one hooked. Flowers red-violet.

POT CULTURE Supply sun, heat and moisture during growing season; light, cool winter, not below 45° to 50° F. Start from seed or offsets. Seedlings may bloom when only an inch high.

HAMATOCACTUS
These small, round plants from Mexico and Texas do very well as house plants. Some species have long, hooked spines (*hamus,* a hook). They are very hardy and not really particular about soil or surroundings.

H. setispinus (Strawberry cactus) Globular to four or five inches, deeply tubercled with a star of white spines on each tip, and tiny dots of white fuzz between high spots. Looks touchable, but be careful; there is one stiff, sharp, hard-to-see central and it sticks straight up. Although a mature plant is about five inches across, a tiny one of little more than an inch will bloom. Flowers are yellow with a red throat. Strawberry-like fruits. (Some taxonomists classify this one in the *Ferocactus* genus.)

H. uncinatus Cylindrical, to eight inches, with very long hooked radial spines which are reddish when young. Centrals to over four inches long! Flowers are small and dull red.

POT CULTURE Hamatocactus are not overly concerned with the finer aspects of care and feeding. Standard cactus procedures will keep them as happy as clams. Propagate from seed.

ASTROPHYTUM
These sun-loving, star-shaped plants from Mexico (*aster:* star, *phytos:* plant) are globular with a few very exaggerated ribs, usually spineless and covered with what looks like a bad case of dandruff. Short, funnel-shaped flowers are borne on the top from new areoles.

Without any encouragement, astrophytums will hybridize quite freely among themselves and some of them have nothing against cozying up to an echinocactus or two. Although astrophytums seem to have no trouble at all finding each other, they can be very tricky about exposing themselves to human eyes. They are hard to see when growing on their home ground, because they tend to pull into the soil when moisture is scarce. Only after a good rain, or when they are in bloom, do they look like plants instead of a lumpy hillside.

Early cactus collectors could get very cagy about the exact location of a colony of astrophytums, preferring to keep the secret to themselves and letting other hunters get eyestrain on their own. Once the plants and their proud collectors were back in Europe, queries such as, "Where did you ever find that?" were met with a vague gesture in the general direction of Mexico. Specimens of *A. asterias* were among the shown-off plants then ... until they died. The discoverer of the species also passed on and *A. asterias* became only a fond memory. It took 100 years to find it again. In 1943 the original growing area was rediscovered, and this time the location was written down, precisely and in triplicate!

A. asterias A collapsed globe with eight broad rounded ribs, gray-green in color and flecked with white spots. A line of large, spineless areoles runs down the center of each rib. Although the cactus grows to about nine inches in diameter in the wild, four or five inches is the average for cultivated plants. The yellow flowers have an orangy throat, and are often bigger than the plant.

A. capricorne Yes, you astrology buffs are right. *Capricorne* does indeed mean goat-horned. This cactus is named for its long, flat, curly spines, which are fragile and easily broken. No rough handling, please. The plant is cylindrical, growing to a foot high, and has eight or nine ribs typically spotted with white scales. Silky pale yellow flowers with an orange-red blotch at the base of the petals often measure three inches across. *A. capricorne* is willing to bloom at a very early age, and just as willing to lose its roots if overwatered.

There are several hybrid forms and varieties of *A. capricorne,* many of which are grafted onto stock that has less touchy roots than the *capricorne* itself.

cv. *'Aureum'* Yellow, young spines and more scales.

cv. *'Majus'* A larger form with no red blotch on the flowers.

cv. *'Minus'* A four-inch plant with small flowers. Papery spines are not as brittle as others.

cv. *'Niveum'* Large, beautiful and covered with white scales.

cv. *'Senile'* Large, very long spines and fewer white spots.

A. myriostigma Common name, Bishop's Cap, for the shape of the plant. This is one of the easiest to grow, having a fairly hardy root system. Blooms readily, too. It is normally five ribbed, although other forms do occur, and becomes cylindrical with age. The skin is dark green and silvered with scales. Large, spineless areoles march down the ribs, giving the plant a buttoned-down look. The flowers are sweet and glossy yellow.

Whether the following plants are *varieties* or *forms* depends on whose opinion you regard as gospel. Part of the problem is that every once in a while one of these plants will confound the experts by doing something different. For example, a four-ribber (var. *quadricostatum*) seedling will often take on a smug expression and grow another rib, which is as good a way as any to blow its *true variety* status. Other varieties (or forms) can show streaks of contrariness, too. I don't know if the *myriostigma* is born balmy or if it's something it picks up later on, out of boredom.

I have listed them as varieties, not forms. No, I don't know for sure which they are. It's just that the "f" key on my typewriter sticks, and the "v" doesn't. They do all have yellow flowers, some with a red base.

var. *coahuilense* An ultimately large plant, to two feet, very densely covered with white scales.

var. *nudum* Dark green and nude, no scales; four ribs, or maybe five.

var. *quadricostatum* A four-ribbed, squared-off cactus with small, clear yellow flowers.

var. *tulensis* Very large, sharp ribs, of which there are usually five, though there can be as many as 10.

A. ornatum This species is not as controversial as the last one and it does not bloom as easily indoors. It usually has to be about six inches high before it will even think about flowers. In its natural setting *A. ornatum* will grow to a yard high and a foot through; no such luck in a pot. The edges of the ribs are sharp and wavy. Spines are few but long, curved and very stout. Silvery scales band the plant and the flowers are large and lemon yellow. It is thought to be a natural hybrid between *A. myriostigma* and an echinocactus. What the heck? You can't watch them all the time! Cv. *Mirbellii* is heavily scaled and sports light yellow spines, while var. *glabrescens* has only a few scales to call its own. Both have yellow flowers.

POT CULTURE Use a very porous soil mix and add some extra lime. Be very careful about your watering habits, especially with the timid-rooted ones if they have not been grafted. Astrophytums definitely do not want wet feet. In the summer they will take all the sun and warmth they can get; in winter keep quite dry and cool (not below 40° F). A healthy, happy plant will usually produce a flower on each new areole as it is formed.

Propagation is from seed, as this cactus does not have offsets. Seeds are large and shell-like, and eager to grow. Germination may occur in 48 hours. If seedlings look sick or are not growing well, chop them off and graft onto a short, stout base.

NOTE
If your interest runs to small, rounded plants, look into the *Parodia, Coryphantha* or *Notocactus* population. They are all neat, attractive plants which will give you no trouble. Lovely flowers, too. I hate to leave them out, but if I included everybody in this book, it would have to be published in installments!

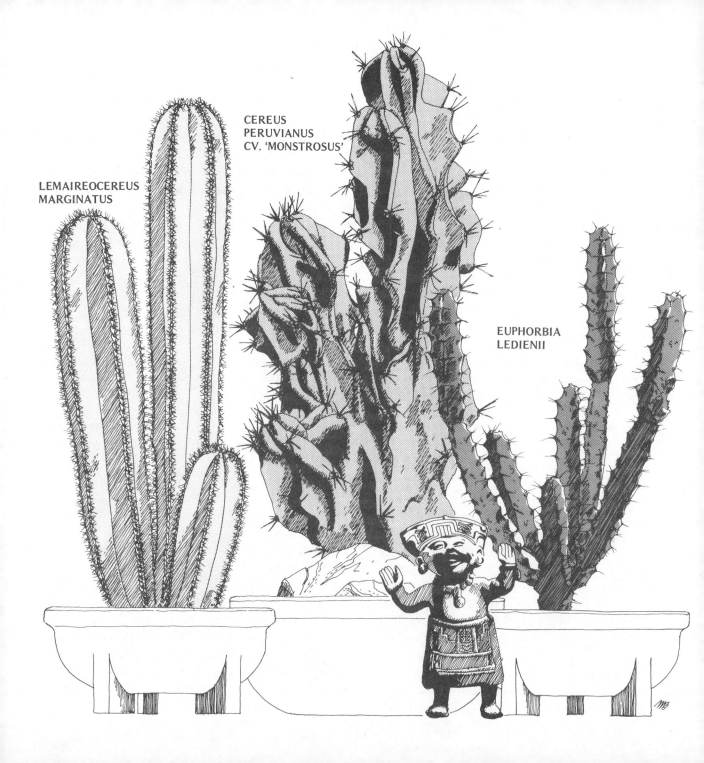

LEMAIREOCEREUS
MARGINATUS

CEREUS
PERUVIANUS
CV. 'MONSTROSUS'

EUPHORBIA
LEDIENII

the well adjusted: columnar

CARNEGIEA GIGANTEA

This species, common name Saguaro, is truly a giant and is the only one in the genus. Saguaros can grow to be some 50 feet tall, and live to be 200 or more years old. They are very slow growers. At age 30, a Saguaro will measure about three feet. At six inches they are already about eight or nine years old. They rarely get "arms" until they are 75 years of age, and if they are in an unfavorable location they may never get them.

Although less than two feet in diameter at the base, a mature Saguaro can weigh several tons—up to seven or so. About 75 percent of their weight is water, which is painstakingly collected by a root system that can reach 100 feet in diameter. Even though the root system is widespread, it is shallow, and windstorms can blow the cactus over.

A Saguaro can unpleat its columnar, bellow-like body by 50 percent to accommodate the moisture gathered during a single rainstorm, and when you realize that a big one can hold up to 600 gallons of water, that's a lot of unpleating. And as a cactus can't say no, if the rains fall long enough the Saguaros will overindulge and bust a gusset when their skin can stretch no more. By the same token, the longer they go without a drink the skinnier they get. Their candelabra arms droop in a forlorn attitude during a long period of no rainfall, but will pop back up again as soon as it rains.

When winter comes, Saguaros shift into over-drive and coast for a couple of months. Those that live near the frost line go into the winter with very little stored moisture and a visibly shriveled appearance. Because water expands when it freezes, a low moisture content minimizes the possiblity that a cold snap could split a Saguaro down the seams.

In April, presuming it has rested well and that it is about 40 years old, the Saguaro puts forth 5-inch-long buds that open to scented, waxy white flowers with fuzzy yellow stamens. By June or July the fruits have ripened, and are commonly used by the Indians of the Southwest to make syrup, jam and wine.

Saguaro seedlings are becoming scarce. Birds, animals and man eat the seeds in large numbers, and the thin, protective layer which covers the desert floor has been disturbed in many areas, making it impossible for seeds to germinate. According to one botanist, out of 40 million seeds only three or four will survive.

POT CULTURE Please do not dig up a Saguaro in the wild! Get one from a dealer who either grows them from seed or by cuttings.

They need extra sharp and gritty soil, and if your plant is any size at all, put it in a container big enough to keep it from becoming top-heavy and falling over. Repot about every four years.

From March to September, water it as often as the soil dries out, and if it is a very small young one, give it some filtered shade on bright, hot days. Keep the plant quite dry in winter, and in a cool location: minimum temperatures of 40° to 45° F.

To start from seed, and it is a very slow proposition, barely cover the seed and keep shaded at about 70° F until the seedling is ready to prick out and transplant. It is ready for this when the cotyledon (first leaves) has been absorbed. Cuttings can be rooted in a very sandy-type rooting mixture.

If you are able to give a Saguaro perfect growing conditions, your grandchildren may live to see it branch.

CEREUS

Once upon a time, if a cactus wasn't a round hedgehog and wasn't an opuntia, it was a cereus. When the number of plants going by that name grew to several hundreds, taxonomists decided to do some hard discriminating and the genus *Cereus* was reduced to about 25 species. Most of the other cereus types were placed in their own genera, which include the largest of all cactus—the 40- to 50-foot Organ-Pipe, *Lemaireocereus Thurberi,* and the 60-footer Cardon, *Pachycereus Pringlei.*

When young, the cereus is a single column, but with age it branches from either near the top or at the base. Spines and ribs vary greatly in number and form, but body color remains blue-green or gray-green throughout the genus. They are all sturdy, vigorous growers, often used as grafting stock for less fortunate cactus with shaky roots. Their large, nocturnal white or pink flowers are seldom seen under cultivation. A few may flower if conditions are ideal, but the fleshy, usually edible fruits don't develop unless you sneak up on the blooms at night with a handful of the right kind of insects.

Cereus are easy to grow and quite striking. They may, in fact, strike the roof. With good care and time, these fellas can get big! For hairy columns, see The Fair-Haired Boys: Cactus.

C. hexagonus Typical gray or blue-green stem color, but hexagonal in shape. Usually spineless.

C. Jamacaru Yellow-spined version of *peruvianus,* which follows. In a bag of mixed seed, both species are most always included.

C. peruvianus (Peruvian tree cactus or Hedge cactus) Tree-like and branching, to 30 or 40 feet, but doesn't often branch indoors unless beheaded. Blue-green stems (new growth is lighter in color) are ribbed and dotted with gray areoles bearing small clusters of spines. Late summer flowers are white, and about six inches long and five across.

C. peruvianus cv. 'Monstrosus' A smaller, slower growing form, with the ribs bent into knobs and bumps. Unusual and attractive.

POT CULTURE Extremely easy to satisfy; give the standard cactus care. Summering the plants outside, in bright, filtered sun, may help out if you are trying for bloom. Propagate from seed.

LEMAIREOCEREUS

Tall, ribbed columns, branching just above the ground. They are native to Arizona and points south, about as far as Peru. Although many lemaireocereus are gigantic, they will do well in a pot and usually stay within bounds; 40-foot plants have yet to grow out of six-inch pots.

Species from the southerly areas are more tropical and need warmer winter temperatures, but other than that they should give you no big headaches. Flowers? Almost non-existent on potted plants. You aren't missing much anyway. They are small and whitish, and not necessary to the enjoyment of these very winning plants.

L. Beneckei Very attractive with few branches, even in their native central Mexico. Radial spines to an inch and a half long, with one reddish central. Light coating of powder on stems. Needs warm winter.

L. Chichipe Ribs rounded and powdered bluish white. New spines reddish. Slow-growing seedlings have the most powder. Needs warm winter.

L. marginatus (Mexican Fence Post or Organ-Pipe) A branching column to 20 feet, often used as a hedge plant in Mexico. Lovely gray-green color and small spines. Seedlings are very effective in dish gardens when planted with a few assorted ball-type cactus. Easy to grow and fairly fast growing. Keep above 45° F in winter.

L. pruinosus (Powder-Blue cereus) Beautiful, ribbed, blue stems. Best color on new growth. White or rosy flowers.

L. Thurberi Many ribbed stems branching freely at the base, eventually making large clumps when grown in open ground. Not nearly so exuberant when potted. Stems are green, sometimes with a purplish cast, and glossy dark spines spike the new growth. Slow growing when small; larger plants put on a little more speed.

POT CULTURE Not as easy as many other cereus types. It is sometimes difficult to maintain a balance between warm-enough-for-comfort, and cool-enough-for-resting. *L. marginatus* is probably the least touchy. Give regular cactus culture during the active growth period.

CHAMAECEREUS SILVESTRI

Commonly called Peanut cactus, and named for Dr. Silvester, a zoologist. Zoologist? Maybe he had been around elephants for too long and was on a peanut kick.

This little plant has been a favorite for many years, and it deserves to be. It is hardy and free flowering, and grows in clusters that don't get out of hand. The soft, pale green stems are ribbed with low tubercles and covered with fine grayish spines. The flowers are a bright, clear red and large for the size of the cactus: up to two inches wide, and high. Because this little Argentinian cactus is a prolific bloomer, it is a boon to growers who have never had much luck trying to bring a cactus into flower.

POT CULTURE Peanut cactus need vitamins to produce all those big flowers, so plant them in rich soil with plenty of grit for fast drainage. Keep them cool and on the dry side in the winter to encourage blooming; in a too warm room they are susceptible to red spider attacks. The stems may take on a reddish hue after being in bright summer sun, which is perfectly normal. In poor light the stems get pale and weedy looking, so provide a nice sunny place to keep the plant short and plump.

This cactus can be hard to repot, not because the spines are a hazard, but because it's difficult to keep the stems from breaking off. Re-root any broken stems and plant them back with the original cactus if you want a big spread; otherwise, pot them up individually and give them to your friends.

57

WHO WAS THAT CACTUS I SAW YOU WITH? Chamaecereus are not too discriminating about who they carry on with; I mean it doesn't necessarily have to be another chamaecereus. A lobivia will do. Then if you introduce an echinopsis to a chamaecereus and a lobivia at the same time, anything can happen. It's more than the odd couple; it's the odd trio! In a situation like this, the offspring could end up not even having a name which is permissible to use in polite society, but in this case they do—Johnson 'Paramount' hybrids.

Sometimes they are called Paramount hybrids and sometimes Johnson hybrids. Don't let that confuse you; they are one and the same. They are easily flowered and just as hardy as their parents ... all of them. The flowers are large and profuse, and there is a nice selection of colors: yellow, pink, red, orange and pastel blends.

When a chamaecereus and a lobivia are left alone together, the hybrids are called *Chamaelopsis*. One of the most popular is *Chamaelopsis* X 'Fire Chief,' a very free-flowering plant with large red flowers.

EUPHORBIA
The genus *Euphorbia* has the largest membership of the family *Euphorbiaceae* (common name spurge). Many of the more than 7,000 species of this family are not succulent, however; they are trees, shrubs and herbs, such as Poinsettias, Chenille plants, Caster-oil plants, Tapioca plants (Cassava). Both the genus and the family name are in honor of Euphorbus, a physician to King Juba of Mauritania.

When you enter the realm of the genus *Euphorbia,* you must prepare yourself for some hostilities.

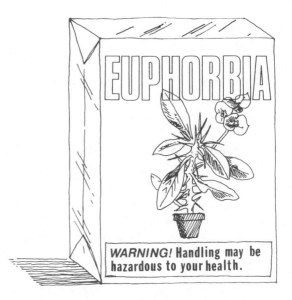

WARNING! Handling may be hazardous to your health.

The first one is the milky sap of these succulents; it is irritating to the skin and eyes. *How* irritating depends on the person, and the plant. Sap will not escape unless the plant is accidentally broken or a cutting is taken. Adults should have no trouble keeping it off their skin; it's as simple as "don't touch the dripping end." Any adult who can't refrain from getting the stuff all over his hands and then sticking a finger in his eye, shouldn't be allowed to eat with a sharp fork, either. If you do happen to catch a drip, wash with warm, soapy water right away and you will suffer no consequences. Keep weeping cuttings in an out-of-the-way place until they dry off; same for the wounded plant.

The second kind of hostile action is of a different sort. Many euphorbias, especially these columnar ones, look almost exactly like cactus, and you may have a hard time convincing some people that they are not. Lack of areoles might not change their opinion, so be prepared for the argument that might ensue.

The diversity of the forms of euphorbias is just too fascinating to pass up. Most of them spend their lives trying to look like something else—anything else. They don't care if it's a cactus, a bush with leaves, or a baseball. Here are some columnar kinds of euphorbias.

E. horrida Columnar to about three feet; rounded in youth. Gray-green with about a dozen narrow, toothy-edged ribs covered with groups of spines about three quarters of an inch long. Aging plants have brown, corky bases. A tough and hardy species. Variety *nova* has a shorter but rougher appearance.

E. ingens Beautiful dark green color, with wavy ribs and "candelabra" growth. Similar to *E. lydenburgensia*, which looks like a pre-shrunk Saguaro cactus.

E. Knobelii Uneven, wavy stems with spines along ribs.

E. Ledienii Spiny, gray-green stems with riblike ridges.

E. submammillaris (Corn Cob, sometimes Corn Cob cactus) A light green, straight-up, branching plant with light brown spines mostly on the top half of the plant. Six-sided, barely raised, flat tubercles give it the corn-on-the-cob look. Off and on, tiny fleshy leaves appear on the new growth. Older plants get a little gray around the bottom. Nondescript flowers are grouped tightly together on the tops of the stems.

POT CULTURE Pretend they are very easy-to-get-along-with cactus and give them the standard soil and sun treatment, but slightly more water. If sunshine is a little scarce, they will adapt to it and do quite well with good bright light. As these fakers are from South Africa, they appreciate warm winters of 50° to 60° F. Water less when they are resting, but don't let them dry out completely. Propagate from seed or stem cuttings.

Other euphorbias under Bushy and Hanging, and The Crazies.

PACHYPODIUM

These spiny succulents are tropicals from South Africa and Madagascar, and belong to the same family as the Oleander and Periwinkle. They were named for their thick, fleshy roots (*pachys*, thick; *podos*, foot). Although the stems are densely covered with pairs of spines, there is a spiral of leaves growing from the top. The combination of a gray cactuslike stem and a whorl of long, green leaves makes them very attractive. Prepare yourself for the inevitable exclamation from visitors: "Gee, I never saw a cactus with leaves on it before!"

P. Lamieri (Madagascar palm) Thickly spined, slightly swollen stem with a topknot of dark green, glossy, narrow, long leaves. Looks like a palm tree.

P. Leadii subsp. *Saundersii* Probably the hardiest. Similar to *Lamieri*, but with a more tapered stem top and shorter leaves.

POT CULTURE Good porous soil with added loam. Because of those leaves, give more water than you would for a cactus, but do it carefully. They are succulent plants with an aversion to wet feet and overwatering. Sun or partial sun. Warmth in winter.

Propagate by cuttings, which should be placed under glass or plastic to ensure roots.

CRASSULA LYCOPODIOIDES

SEDUM
MORGIANIANUM

AEONIUM
ARBOREUM

the well adjusted: bushy and hanging

SEDUM

Though most familiar as outdoor rock garden plants, many sedums are tropical and tender, and very happy to be inside the house. The name *Sedum* is from *sedo,* meaning to sit. Some of these succulents "sit" or grow on rocks, and are often used as a ground cover. The species mentioned here, however, would rather dig into a pot and grow into small shrubs.

S. amecamecanum (Mexican Sedum) Yellow-green leaves on densely branched stems, about eight inches high. Yellow flower clusters in spring and summer. Sometimes sold as, and confused with, *S. confusum* (with a name like that, the plant is asking for it). *S. confusum* is taller, about a foot high, and larger leafed; one-and-a-half-inch oval leaves in light green. Late spring clusters of yellow flowers.

S. Morganianum cv. 'Baby Burro's-Tail' Cultivar of the old favorite, Burro's-Tail; with its three-foot-long ropes of blue-green, fat leaves. "Baby" is much smaller and shorter; tiny light green, grape-like leaves. Hanging stems are not as even and symmetrical as those of the bigger one. A dainty plant for hanging.

S. multiceps (Baby Joshua Tree) A good minia-ture "tree" for bonsai or dish garden plantings. Compact and many branched, with tight clusters of dark green, very tiny succulent leaves. Small yellow flowers. Summer dormant.

S. X rubrotinctum Sprawling or hanging stems to about eight inches long. Jelly beanlike leaves, light green with reddish tips; sun will intensify red color. Small flowers are reddish yellow.

S. Stahii (Coral Beads) Branching stems with very closely set, translucent-looking leaves. With plenty of sun, the plant takes on a reddish color. To about eight inches high.

POT CULTURE Let soil go dry before watering again; these plants do not like constant dampness. If leaves start to lose their fat, ripe look, and shrivel, you are keeping them too dry. Give them a sunny place for good leaf color and a gritty soil for healthy growth. Once a month fertilizing during growing season. These sedums are not cold hardy; 50° to 60° F minimum temperature.

Propagate by stem cutting or by individual leaf. Species with small bean-type leaves will shed when bumped, dropping a dozen potential plants in one shot. Either keep the plant in a protected place or be prepared to furnish the neighborhood with sedum "starts."

AEONIUM

These are members of the crassula family from the Canary Islands and the Mediterranean area. Many of them resemble the garden plant Hen-and-Chicks, but instead of hugging the ground they grow tall (to three feet) and branched. Flowers are small but produced in long clusters on a stalk.

A. arboreum Six- to eight-inch rosettes, light green and slightly fringed, on branched stems to about three feet tall. Yellow flowers. *S. arboreum* var.

atropurpureum has dark purple leaves and the cultivar 'Zwartkop' has purple-black leaves.

A. ciliatum Many stems with leaves rounded, pointed at tips. Greenish-white flowers.

A. decorum Bushy plants to about a foot high with two-inch rosettes of reddish leaves. Compact, rounded plant; light pink flowers.

A. Haworthii Bluish-green compact rosettes with red edges on branching stems to two feet. Cream-colored or rose-tinged flowers.

POT CULTURE Porous succulent soil. If mixing your own from "regular" potting soil, add very coarse sand or grit; mixture must be very sharp and fast draining. Sun or bright diffused light. Water when soil is dry through growing period; less often in winter. Minimum temperature 45° F.

Propagate by seed or stem or leaf cutting.

CRASSULA (Hanging)
C. brevifolia Similar to *perforata*, below, but smaller and more delicate.

C. lycopodioides (Watch Chain) Four rows of closely growing tiny green leaves on branching stems. Stems erect while short, flopping when longer. Looks like moss or coral.

C. perforata Shrubby and pendant, with fleshy stems measured off in pairs of joined leaves. Leaves are pale greenish gray, broad and pointed at the tips. In good light they have a red border and reddish mini-dots. Small whitish flowers. Several hybrids available, which are less spreading.

X 'Jade Necklace' A hybrid with very tightly packed leaves, much more compact.

CRASSULA (Upright)
The old favorite, Jade plant *(C. argentea)*, has been picked apart and put back together in almost every house plant book ever written. And it still remains a favorite! I don't suppose the fact that it's versatile, adaptable, hardy and looks great, has anything to do with it. But, now there are a couple of other versions.

C. argentea cv. 'Crosby' (Mini Jade) Same dark green succulent leaves and form as the original, but more compact, denser, smaller. A beauty for Oriental dish gardens or single plantings where space is lacking.

C. argentea cv. 'Variegata' Same form and size with highlights of cream striping the leaves.

Another small, robust crassula is the hybrid 'Brides Bouquet.' Unlike the *argentea*, whose star-like flowers rarely show up indoors, this plant is in bloom most of the time. It is thickly branched and leafed in dark green. A dwarf, usually covered with very small, waxy white flowers. Tight and rounded like a nosegay. Very hardy.

POT CULTURE Crassulas will survive in less than good light, but for best growth and leaf color they need some sun; a few hours each day will do, they don't want to be baked. Use porous soil and water only when dry. More water is indicated if leaves look limp or leathery. Partial sun, dry, cool conditions in winter, but not too cold. Remember these are tropical or near-tropical plants.

PORTULACARIA

This is a succulent member of the purslane family, from South Africa and is similar to the Jade plant in structure.

P. afra (Elephant bush, Elephant's Food or Purslane tree) Evidently, elephants go for these juicy shrubs, but I couldn't find out for sure without making a personal observation ... and a trip to Africa to see what elephants eat for breakfast isn't included in my research budget. Under cultivation the *P. afra* isn't big enough to get hung-up between a pachyderm's toes, but in its native soil it grows to 12 feet high and just about as wide; big enough for a snack, at least.

If you are not troubled by grazing animals, you can count on a medium-sized, juicy-stemmed plant, branching like a small tree. The trunk gets brown and leathery looking, like the Jade plant, as it grows older. Fast growing, limber branches will eventually cascade, making it an effective hanging-pot plant. Small oval leaves and pink flowers. Flowers are rarely produced under cultivation.

P. afra cv. *'Tricolor'* or *P. afra* cv. *'Folius Variegatis'* (Rainbow bush) Dwarf, many-branched version with yellow, green, pink or cream leaf colors. Slower growing.

POT CULTURE Same culture as Jade plant: water when soil has dried; partial sun or very bright light and cooler, drier winters. Quite hardy, in spite of its delicate look. Propagate by cuttings; they root easily.

EUPHORBIA

Another old standby (I'm sure early man lugged one from cave to cave) is the Crown-of-Thorns, *Euphorbia Milii* var. *splendens.* Its gray, spiny stems, green leaves and ever-blooming two-petaled red flowers make it an attractive house plant. The only thing wrong with it is that it often outgrows its welcome, becoming an impenetrable hedge along the window. The dwarf species are safer and easier to house and are also good bonsai specimens.

E. Bojeri Very compact and leafy, and does not sprawl. Dark red flowers.

E. Milii var. *imperatae* Its spiny stems have tiny oval leaves of bright green which may shed in the winter. Red flowers bloom constantly, with or without leaves.

POT CULTURE Bright light with some sun. Allow to dry between waterings, but don't let soil ball dehydrate completely; those leaves need moisture for their support. Fertilize lightly about once a month during the growing season, but never in winter. Poor air circulation and high temperatures may bring on a mealy bug or spider mite siege. Prune to bonsai form if you wish, but be careful of the milky sap. Propagate by cuttings.

More euphorbias in The Well-Adjusted: Columnar, and The Crazies.

PILOSOCEREUS
PALMERI

MAMMILLARIA
BOCASANA

the fair-haired boys: cactus

It's an even bet that if a cactus grower could have only two plants, one of them would be hairy. A plant with hair has irresistible appeal. The Old Man cactus is the most popular and one of the shaggiest, but there are others with hair down to their ankles, not as well known maybe, but just as attractive. Other cactus family members are covered with short, soft hair and they look like white fuzzy balls, while still others are cotton edged and topped. A few of them are not white, though most of them are.

OLD AGE IS WHAT IT IS
New, young growth has the whitest hair. In many species, those of the cereus group in particular, the hair gets yellowish with age and the plant may also look a little scruffy around the bottom. It's a natural maturing process and nothing can be done about it without resorting to radical surgery. Some people cut the tops off of these older plants and re-root them, leaving the bottom half to re-sprout with new growth. This beheading will assure youthful, white-haired stems that are the pride and joy of some growers.

The maturing of these cactus doesn't bother me too much; some of us humans don't age all that gracefully either. I mean, if a little scruffy hair and a slightly moth-eaten body really offended me, I'd never be able to look into a mirror again. Then, too, I'd like to see if I can get my shaggy old goat of a cactus to bloom. Usually, about the time this plant is mature enough to flower, somebody whacks the top off and that's one of the reasons why the cereus types seldom flower as potted plants.

WHO NEEDS A DIRTY OLD MAN?
Aged fading is one thing; dust and air-borne grime is another. Most people don't want a dirty old man around the house, at least not a botanical one. If your hairy friend looks dingy, give it a bath. Spray it with warm, soapy water, rinse it off and put it in a shady spot to dry. Do it in the morning so the plant will have a chance to dry before evening rolls around. A hair dryer can be used to dry it off, but back off a bit and don't use a "hot" setting. If the temperature is too hot the plant may be dehydrated severely, not to mention the possibility

of getting split ends. Drying the plant with a jet-like blast of air may also cause a bouffant or Afro hairdo, neither of which is natural to the cactus. In some species of long-hairs the hair hangs down; in others it wraps around. Don't try to rearrange it. These plants do not care about the latest styles.

A COUPLE OF SPECIAL REQUESTS
White-haired cactus like extra lime in their soil; many of them grow naturally in chalky or slate-type soils which are quite alkaline. There are several ways to acquire lime for your cactus and I have listed them in the discussion of soil. They range all the way from boiling eggs to ripping out the concrete foundation of your house.

The hairier the cactus, the more sun it can take. Lots of bright sun seems to help keep white-haired cactus fetchingly snowy. It acts like a bleach job, I guess.

Many of the cactus in this group are from the mountains, and they will expect a fairly dry, cool winter rest. Some of the others are tropical lowlanders, and while they do need their sleep, they don't want to get frostbite at the same time. The natural growing conditions and locations of each species will give you a clue as to what's what.

If you lean toward whitish plants, including those without hair, see *Lemaireocereus Benecke* and *L. Chichipe* and the *Astrophytum* genus in general.

The cereus types featured here as hairy or fuzzy also have naked forms. See "Well Adjusted Columnar."

66

cereus-type hairy cactus

CEPHALOCEREUS

As much as I like this famous Old Man, I wish I had never delved into his past. He comes from a long line of mass confusion! For years, taxonomists have run amok through this genus—adding, subtracting, dividing and squarerooting. They have finally split the large, old genus into three questionable smaller ones and the divisions go like this . . . maybe.

The Old Man cactus from Mexico is the star of the *Cephalocereus* group. Cephalocereus (*kephale:* head) are ribbed, columnar, seldom-branching, woolly topped cactus. Long hair, silky and white, covers the plant when it is young; then it goes bald from the bottom up when it is old and eventually ends up with only a specialized woolly head, or cephalium, on the top few feet. The nocturnal flowers are formed in the cephalium.

Austrocephalocereus are former *Cephalocereus* from South America, mainly Brazil and Bolivia. At first glance the name leads us to believe that these free-branching plants are from Australia and we may think the taxonomists not only need a new Latin grammar, they need a map. Actually, *australis* means southern, and sure enough South America is south of Mexico, and unless continental drift speeds up considerably, it will probably stay there. These warm-growing tropicals are smaller than the *Cephalocereus* species and they dislike winter temperatures below 50° F.

Pilosocereus is a fairly recent name, replacing the old one of *Pilocereus* (*pilosus:* covered with hair). This contains some cactus that used to be included with the *Cephalocereus,* until it was discovered that they were faking it: Ordinary areoles were growing the hair on top (pseudocephalium) and passing themselves off as the real thing (cephalium).

Are you still with me? The only reason I brought this subject up at all was because some of the cactus in this hairy bunch are still called by two names. It may be *Cephalocereus Palmeri* on one list and *Pilosocereus Palmeri* on another, or *Cephalocereus senilis* one place and *Pilocereus senilis* someplace else.

I know you aren't going to go into a frenzy because your whatsis *senilis* has the wrong kind of areoles. I just thought you should know that these old men became senile with good reason; they couldn't stand the pace. Then there's this other thing. . . .

HAVE YOU CHECKED OUT THE BELFRY?

It is often said that *Cephalocereus* and *Austrocephalocereus,* in the wild, are pollinated by the vampire bat. While I've never witnessed the intimate relations of these particular cactus—they deserve some privacy—I'm inclined to think that this is another instance where taxonomy has foiled us. Genuine, blood-lapping vampire bats are not plant lovers; they can't cope with anything except a diet of blood due to their specialized digestive tracts. So, unless cactus flower nectar contains a large amount of plasma, what's in it for them?

Then how did the story get started? Very easily! A mixup with the scientific names. True vampire bats belong to the *Desmodontidae* (band-tooth) group: genus *Desmodus* from Mexico to Chile; genus *Diphylla* in Brazil. Ok, no cause for confusion so far. Fruit-eating bats are more likely to be cactus-flower oriented, and there's this one particular fruit bat which is often mistaken for the true vampire. It belongs to the genus *Vampyrus,* a genus which faints at the sight of blood! The logic behind the choice of this generic name eludes me. Until I can get in touch with Count Dracula, don't feel you have to jump into a bat costume and grow fangs if you want to pollinate your cactus.

Cephalocereus chrysacanthus (Yellow Torch or Golden Old Man Cactus) Columnar, light green stems to 15 feet. Golden yellow hair and spines, and rose nocturnal flowers. From Mexico.

C. leucocephalus Another Mexican cereus with woolly, long hair.

C. senilis (Old Man cactus) In its native Mexico it may live to be 200 years old and some 40 feet tall. At about 20 feet it will lose its lower hair and develop a distinctive woolly head. Young ones are pale green beneath the 20 or 30 long, white hairs grown in each areole. Healthy plants will produce hair as long as five inches. White, nocturnal flowers of a mature plant are seldom seen when grown indoors.

Astrocephalocereus Dybowskii Free branching cactus growing to 12 feet in its native country. It is covered with short, silky, white hairs and looks like a tall cotton ball. Protruding spines.

A. lehmannianus A six foot, bluish-stemmed plant with dense white spines and wool.

Pilosocereus flavilanatus Similar to *P. Palmeri* but, as the name implies, yellow *(flavens)* wool *(lana)*.

P. Palmeri A warm valley cactus from Mexico which forms a branching column about 15 feet high. Areoles produce long, white hair, especially on the flowering side of the stem. Flowers are pink and nocturnal. Often called Woolly Torch cactus. With age, the yellow spines turn black.

P. Royenii A columnar plant with many ribs and both spines and hair along the edges of the ribs.

Note: The *Pilosocereus* are not a mass of hair; they are cottony in varying degrees, depending on the species, along the rib margins. The effect is very striking.

POT CULTURE The cephalocereus group likes a good, porous soil mix. In hot weather, water as often as the soil dries out. If the plants are quite tall, make sure they are in a heavy, solid-bottomed pot for stability. These white-haired cereus are from warm, inland areas; they like lots of sun and semi-cool winters of not less than 45° to 50° F. They are not as cold hardy as many other cactus.

Older specimens take on a natural discoloration, a yellowing. If it bothers you, cut off the top and re-root it for silver-white hair. The bottom part will usually sprout several new stems, all cleanly white haired.

Branching species can be propagated by stem cuttings; otherwise, single stems are beheaded. Many species can be raised from seed, but it takes years before they get to any size at all. All of them are very slow growing and the very young ones have no hair.

CLEISTOCACTUS

This vigorously growing plant was named for its flowers. *Kleistos* means closed: The flowers form along one side of the stem and are shaped like slender tubes that barely open. The plant will come to flower in a pot, but it's a rare day when one will bloom while it is less than four or five feet high. The stems of this cactus are slender and branch at the base to form a cluster. They are worth growing for their beauty without considering the flowers.

C. Ritteri White and hairy with lemon-yellow flowers.

C. Strausii (Silver Torch cactus) A narrow column when young, clustering with age. Beautiful, short silvery hair with a soft fuzzy look. Dark red flowers.

POT CULTURE Cleistocactus need strong light in summer to keep hair in good condition. Standard watering treatment for cactus in summer and winter. Propagation by seed, which grows easily, or stem cutting.

ECHINOCEREUS

Spiny fruit is responsible for the hedgehog *(echinos)* name given to these plants from Mexico and the southern United States. These hardy plants, with their magnificent flowers, are divided into three groups: plants with weak spines; prostrate, mat-forming plants; and erect plants, branching from the base.

Naming these plants has been very difficult for the taxonomists because the cactus can't seem to decide what it wants to look like. I mean it's not too unusual to find one with a purple flower on one side of the stem and a yellow one on the other. Some species change their characteristics when they change scenery; the one growing over here doesn't necessarily look like the one growing over there. They give botanists fits. And I'd say it's high time something did.

E. Delaetii This hairy cereus from Mexico, with red spines on top, looks like the Old Man except that the hair is not as white. It belongs to the erect group and grows at about the 7,000-foot level. The flowers are pale pink and more than two inches across, but the plant doesn't often bloom when house bound, especially in northern localities where it doesn't get enough sun.

POT CULTURE Plant in a very gritty, porous soil and don't allow it to stay damp or it will rot at the roots. Needs plenty of sunshine, and like most mountain cactus, a cool winter rest. Seed grows easily or root stem cuttings.

ESPOSTOA

These white-haired cereus grow in the Andes of Peru and were named for Nicholas Esposto, a botanist from Lima. The plants are slow growing, eventually reaching about 12 feet in height. They are mature at two or three feet and bear whitish flowers, followed by a white, juicy, edible fruit.

The first species and the last species are classified by some as *Espostoa*, and by others as *Thrixanthocereus*. I picked *Espostoa* because it's easier to spell.

E. Blossfeldiorum Very seldom branches; usually columnar with light radial spines having dark-colored, long centrals. White flowers.

E. lanata (Peruvian Old Man cactus) This one was discovered in the early 1800's, then promptly lost for 36 years until somebody stumbled onto it again. The stems have from 20 to 30 low ribs, which are densely covered with areoles. The areoles bear fine white hairs that wrap around the plant. It has radial yellowish-brown spines, and the two- to three-inch-long flowers are borne in a woolly cephalium. There are several varieties and natural hybrids of *E. lanata,* most of them not as branched or as bushy as the true form.

E. melanostele White haired with yellow spines protruding through. Nicest hair is on new growth; on lower stem it turns dark (*melan:* dark).

E. senilis Also usually unbranched, but covered with gleaming white spines.

POT CULTURE These plants have a tendency to rot easily at the base; use a gravel mulch and water carefully. *E. lanata* is sometimes grafted onto a strong, short understock to avoid the rot problem. All species can be cut off and re-rooted to keep whitest hair going. Propagate by stem cutting; seed will grow, but it's a very slow ball game. Other than being careful about watering, give these plants the standard cactus care.

LOPHOCEREUS

These cactus hail from Arizona and Mexico, where they grow along the bottoms of sandy valleys. They are columnar plants that branch from the base and form clumps in their old age. *Lophocereus* (*lophos:* crest or tuft of hair) are nocturnal bloomers, with flowers ranging from white to pink to red. They reach 15 feet in height in the wild, but it is a long, slow process. (One species, *L. australis,* may make it to 25 feet.) The stems of these cactus are angled and covered with brown or grayish, very thick, hairy spines that make the plant look like the tail of a cat who has just been surprised by a large, angry dog.

L. Schottii A stout species, not as slender as the others in this genus (some of them have to be propped up when grown as a single stem in cultivation). There is a monstrous form of this cactus, as bald as its brother is hairy, which has no ribs or spines and looks like a green candle that has dripped and run into a series of knobs and lumps. These monstrosities come from Baja California, where whole colonies of them go mad together. They show no tendency to go straight, which is an oddity because most fasciated cactus have a strong normal growth that has to be taken off, or it will overcome the abnormal part.

L. Sargentianus and *L. australis* are similar to *L. Schottii,* but are more slender.

POT CULTURE These cactus like plenty of sun and a rich, porous soil. Water well in summer; give standard winter treatment of cool, dry rest. Propagate by stem cutting; seed is *very* slow.

OREOCEREUS

Sounds like a cookie, but *oreos* means mountain and that's where these cactus live. (This genus is also called *Borzicactus* with some frequency, another example of cactus authorities trying to confuse us.) They are from the dry eastern slopes of the Andes at altitudes of 10,000 feet and as they are exposed to temperatures below freezing, they begin the winter in a very dry state. (This dehydrated state saves their lives; standing around jolly and waterlogged would be a foolhardy move in winter, as they would immediately turn into icicles.) The amount of white hair varies from one species to another, depending on the altitude and how much of a fur coat each one will need. Oreocereus branch freely from the base and form lumps with maturity, and as with most other woolly cactus, the lower parts of the stem become a little mangy with age. Their flowers are red and on the small side.

O. Celsianus (Old-Man-of-the-Mountains) Will grow to about three feet in cultivation. Long, silky hair with light brownish-yellow spines. Young ones have a wild appearance; the hair on top sticks up in a bunch of cowlicks.

O. fossulatus The amount of hair this species produces when potted varies quite a bit; usually the better the light, the better the crop. Long brownish spines.

O. Ritteri Yellow spines and abundant white wool.

O. Trolli Grows slowly to about three feet or so. This troll is covered with whitish-gray wool with embedded reddish-colored spines.

POT CULTURE They should be kept much drier than most cactus in the winter, and cooler, about 40° to 45°F when potted. Water sparingly in the summer and give them lots of sun. Propagate from seed or by stem cuttings.

WILCOXIA

Named for General Timothy Wilcox, who has been described as a "keen student of plants." The plants in this genus have slender stems and a tuberous root. Their growth is stunted unless potted in a large container, so they are often grafted onto a cereus stem, giving a candelabra look to the finished product. The flowers are purplish pink and large for the size of the stems. Native to Mexico and Texas.

W. Schmollii Sometimes called *W. senilis*. The stems of this species are thicker and shorter than other wilcoxias, but still quite slender. (Others are about the size of a pencil.) Stems are covered with short, soft, white hair and it makes a striking plant when grafted onto a tall base.

POT CULTURE If grafted, give it the standard cactus treatment: sun, water when dry, cool rest in winter. If the plant is growing on its own root, then it must have a pot large enough to contain the tuber. In cultivation it grows better and faster when grafted. Propagate by stem cuttings.

other hairy cactus

MAMMILLARIA

This is another genus that botanists and taxonomists keep fiddling with, not because they are trying to get it to clean up its act (like the *Echinocereus*), but because they think there are just too darn many mammillarias. The *Abbey Garden Catalogue* lists 190 of them, and that's just a drop in the bucket. Some of the scientific people have divided them into two groups: plants with watery sap and plants with milky sap. Others disagree with this type of classification because they have found that some species have watery sap at one time of the year and milky sap at another. Still others have decided that they have better things to do than sit around sticking pins into a cactus to see what comes out, and they ignore the whole business. "Let's face it," they say, "this happens to be a horrendously big genus."

Mammillarias are covered with little bumps, or tubercles, not ribs. (*Mamillia:* nipple.) Spines grow from the tips of these bumps and although they are variable in size and shape, the common name, Pincushion cactus, is fitting. The plants are low growing and often clustering, with small bell-shaped flowers borne in circlets around the top. They bloom on old areoles, which means the plant must do well one year to flower the next.

Most of these plants come from Mexico, with a sparse scattering of them spreading north and south of this country. Local people pick the fruit of some species and eat them like berries. Unlike most cactus, mammillarias will often set seed as house plants if they are helped along by insects or by humans. They can be hand pollinated by using a little brush to dab the flowers. If you have more than one species blooming at the same time, clean the brush before going on to the next plant or you may have some very haphazard hybrids coming up from the seed. Those of you who are smirking could care less about this. You devils!

Non-hairy mammillarias can be found in Well Adjusted: Globular.

In a genus this large there is a plant to suit growers in any stage of green thumbery—from the fast growing, easy and indestructible species to the difficult and touchy. The types with hooked spines may not be the easiest of the lot, but they are nothing to get hysterical about either.

M. bocasana (Powder-Puff cactus) This is one of the most popular cactus grown. It is bluish green and covered with silky-white radial spines. The central spines are hooked, but luckily it is still an easy grower. The creamy yellow flowers are profuse, but small. Start with one little cushion of this cactus and you'll soon have a cluster of them.

M. candida The most beautiful mammillaria, but not the easiest to grow as it is very prone to rotting off at the neck. In its native Mexico it grows in chalky soil, which is alkaline in composition. The plant is covered thickly with fine, compressed, white spines and the total effect is fuzzy rather than hairy. The early summer flowers are white with a faint pink stripe. The varieties *rosea* (rosy central spines) and *caespitosa* are gorgeous.

M. Hahniana (Old Lady cactus) A globular, spiny, long-haired plant with a name that sounds like a fit of nervous giggles. It does not cluster as quickly as *M. bocasana,* remaining solitary while youthful. It has a grayish-green stem and up to 30 short, interlacing, white radial spines growing from each areole. Long hair grows from between the tubercles in varying lengths of up to two inches. Pink to red flowers and red fruit with brown seeds inside.

M. plumosa A white mound of separate heads which are very hard to distinguish. Feathery white spines that are radial and numerous; white flowers.

M. Schwarzii A small, clustering, fuzzy-ball type.

POT CULTURE The white-haired members of this genus are usually not too tricky to grow if you give them a very porous, fast-draining soil and don't overwater them. Most of them need direct sun, although the hooked-spined species seem to like a bit of shade. Cool, dry winter rest is essential to all of them. Seeds germinate easily, and seedlings are fairly fast growing. Offsets, rooted in sand, will bloom within a season or so. Don't expect bloom on a plant you abused last year; yesterday's healthy areoles are today's flowers.

MAMILLOPSIS

These plants from the mountains of Mexico are one of the *opsis* or "looks like" cactus types. The confusion about the classification of mammillarias is understandable; there are so many species. Classification of the *Mamillopsis* is confusing, too, but for a different reason. In this genus there are only two species! Or is it one species and one variety? I certainly don't know which it is, and it seems that I'm not the only one.

M. senilis A small, round, fluffy, silver-white ball that some think is the most beautiful cactus Mexico has to offer. Snowball cactus would be a good name for it. It does often winter under snow, in a very, very dry condition. A mature plant will cluster and each head will eventually get to be about three inches across. The flowers are red and large, nearly two inches across. A spectacular plant when it blooms! Semi-spectacular when it doesn't!

That questionable other plant? *M. Diguetti.* Or, var. *Diguetti*? It has smaller, orange flowers and stouter spines. Attractive and rare.

POT CULTURE Plant in standard succulent soil with gravel added to insure good drainage, and take care not to overwater, particularly in the winter. You don't have to bury it in a snow bank, just keep it cool, about 45°F, and rested for a while during the winter months. Propagate from offsets of plants old enough to cluster, or seed.

OPUNTIA

These are the cactus with the glochids, those little barbed spines, so don't be tempted to pet their hairy little heads.

O. erinacea (Grizzly-Bear cactus) A California flat-padded cactus with long, hairy spines. Flowers yellow to red.

O. floccosa A small South American cactus, with joints up to six inches long covered with a silky, white coat of hair. In their native land they are alpines and they grow right up to the snow line.

POT CULTURE Well watered in the summer and not allowed to dry out completely in the winter. Details under genus *Opuntia* section.

CRASSULA

DUDLEYA

the fair-haired boys: succulents

Other succulents may not have the shaggy-mop look of some cactus, but there are some pale and plush ones, some silvery-white ones and a few that are chalk powdered. There are even a couple with hairy flowers, and you can hardly beat that. Any of these pallid plants will make a startling addition to your collection, and some of them do not require abundant amounts of bright sun, as the cactus do.

With the exception of the kinds with powdered leaves, no special care is needed: standard succulent culture will keep them healthy and happy. Not that the powdery ones are so all-fired picky; they just don't like to be touched or watered from overhead. It ruins the look of their chalk-dusted leaves, and after having one around for a while, you'll get just as vain about their beauty as they are. "Don't touch that plant!" becomes the common battle cry, often giving visitors who thought you were quite reserved a terrible fright. These plants can *not* be sprayed or bathed; dust must be gently blown off. Keep them looking their best.

Fuzzy, plush succulents can be cleaned with a soft brush or bathed with warm water and soap. Don't dry them in direct sun or they'll get a spotty sunburn.

Note: Several genera fall into more than one of the following sections, depending on species.

WARNING
All of the plants in the pale and plush, silvery, and powdered sections belong to the crassula family. Do not use any bug spray with the ingredient Malathion in it in the vicinity of crassulas. If you must spray some of your other plants, remove the members of this family from the premises. The chalky or powdered types can't be sprayed with anything; it would wreck the makeup job.

pale and plush

The succulents in this pale and plush group range from definitely hairy to barely fuzzed. All are members of the crassula family.

COTYLEDON
This African genus is named for its cuplike leaves (*kotyle:* a cavity or cup), although the species listed here are not what I'd call cupped. They have thick, almost flat leaves, with little "toes" on the tips. This fat, flat-footed look has led to several confusing common names.

The hair on these plants is very fine and very short, giving them a soft, velvety look. They are neat, compact and easy to care for; they also like to be petted.

C. ladismithiensis (Bare Foot cactus) A fat-toed species, and certainly not a cactus. A more delicate, paler green than the *tomentosa* that follows.

C. teretifola Soft hairs on pale green, almost cylindrical leaves about four inches long. This one is less of a foot fetish candidate than the others.

C. tomentosa (Bear Feet) A bushy little plant with downy, clear green leaves. By "clear," I don't mean you can see through them. I mean they are a nice un-gunked shade of green and are very similar to the Bare Foot cactus.

POT CULTURE Bright diffused light or a half day of sunshine daily will keep these plants in good shape. If the new growth starts to "string out," move the plant to a sunnier location; they should stay compact and thickly leafed. Pot in standard succulent mix and from spring to fall water as often as the soil dries out. Less water is needed in winter, but not a complete drought, please. If kept too dry the lower leaves may start dropping. Leaf cuttings taken in the summer will readily root. Although these plants are grown for their foliage, they occasionally put forth yellowish flowers.

There are a couple of odd cotyledons in The Crazies section.

ECHEVERIA
A genus of plants most prevalent in Mexico but native from Texas to Argentina. They grow in orderly rosettes and are named for a botanical draftsman who labored over the volume *Flora Mexicana* in 1858. Echeverias have very symmetrical forms and fascinating leaves that are often marked with reds and pinks or blues and purples. Some species produce chalky-white leaves and some have hair. The reason for the diversity of coloration is due partly to the fact that echeverias have always been very free with their favors, and without any outside help they will hybridize among themselves and with pachyphytums (offspring are *Pachyveria*). With the additional help of humans, the number of species and hybrids has grown to astounding proportions. If you want to grow one of each type, you had better rent a warehouse, maybe two. In the meantime, you might want to try a furry one.

E. Derenbergii X 'Doris Taylor' A white-fuzzed hybrid with dark green, red-tipped leaves.

E. setosa (Mexican Firecracker) A stemless little rosette (about four inches across) with narrow, dark green, densely set leaves and covered with stiff, white, bristle-like hairs. The common name comes from the red-tipped yellow flowers.

POT CULTURE Bright light and some sun are advised for best leaf color. Because these plants are susceptible to cold (minimum 50° F), in severe winter areas don't keep them right up against a window. Standard succulent care and soil. Prone to root rot; water wisely. Propagate from offsets.

KALANCHOE

Kalanchoe (from the Chinese name of one species) are native to the tropical areas of America, Africa and Asia.

K. beharensis (Felt plant) Grows to a great size, up to 10 feet, possibly. Usually unbranched with leaves from four to eight inches long, and thickly coated with white to brown felty hairs. Crimped leaf edges. There are many hybrids in this species, differing in size, shape of leaf and amount of fuzz.

K. tomentosa (Panda plant) The most often seen and grown. It is a shrubby, branching plant with fleshy leaves covered in dense, silvery-white hairs. The leaf tips are serrated and marked with rust spots when young; dark brown with age. They can be had in regular size (to about a foot and a half), dwarf and giant forms. The word *tomentosa* means covered with short, soft, matted, woolly hairs.

POT CULTURE As these plants are tropicals, they do not like to be blistered in the sun or to be dry. Use a fertile, porous planting mix, water them frequently and give them a partially sunny location. Easily propagated by leaf cuttings or seed.

silvery

There may be some difference of opinion over which plants belong in this category and which plants belong in the next (chalky). I will take my chances, however, and risk being trounced in a dark alley some night by those who disagree. The plants I call "silvery" may be filmed over with a white coating, but it is light enough to let the leaf color show through, whereas the ones in the next section are dead white and heavily powdered.

If I were committing the crime of the century, I wouldn't stop on my way out and fondle the foliage of any plant in either group. They are all a fingerprinter's delight.

COTYLEDON

C. orbiculata A shrubby, compact plant with rounded, red-edged leaves. Leaf color may vary from silver-green to gray-green. Flowers are borne in clusters on tall stems; orange and bell-shaped. *C. orbiculata* var. *oophylla* has very small, egg-shaped leaves.

CRASSULA

C. arborescens In its native Africa, this plant is treelike *(arborescens)*, growing to 12 feet; in the house settle for a small shrub. The leaves are large and oval and definitely cupped, with red margins and red dots on silvery green.

C. arborescens var. *glauca* is smaller and bushier and goes by the common name Cookie plant. You can't get much more common than that!

C. deltoidea (Silver-Beads) Low growing, with fleshy whitish, triangular leaves.

POT CULTURE Partial shade or full sun; strong light necessary for good leaf color and red highlights. Water when soil goes dry, but don't make it wait too long; it likes more moisture than most succulents. White-fading-to-pink, star-shaped flowers of the *arborescens* usually are seen only on old, often pot-bound plants. Propagate by leaf or terminal cuttings.

ECHEVERIA
E. elegans (Hen-and-Chickens or Mexican Snowball) Spreading clusters of tight rosettes with light-colored, blue-green, white-frosted leaves, three to six inches across. Pink flowers.
E. glauca var. *pumila* A tight, stemless, frosty blue-gray rosette.

KALANCHOE
K. pumila (Purple and Powder plant) I wish I knew who made up these names! No, the plant isn't purple. It's a frosted blue-green with notched leaves and purplish flowers. The *pumila* is small, branched and compact. How it ever manages to look untidy I'll never know, but it does.

POT CULTURE For the silvery cotyledon, echeveria and kalanchoe, see pale and plush section. Overhandling can botch up the leaves of the plants in this silvery group; normal plant-keeping and general fooling around shouldn't do them any harm. They are not nearly as touchy as their pampered relatives with the snowy coats are.

powdered

The plants in this group are strikingly beautiful and they know it. Their powdered leaves demand careful, clean culture. This pampering applies only to their fancy clothes; underneath it all they are just as hardy as any other succulent. The thick, chalky coating is a protective device which reflects blistering sun, reduces evaporation and discourages animals with a bad case of the munchies.

DUDLEYA
D. Brittonii An 18-inch-wide rosette on a stem which eventually gets trunklike. Looks like a monster chrysanthemum blossom with pure white, fleshy petals.
D. pulverulenta Sometimes called by the common name Chalk Lettuce. Very similar to the above species; maybe a little bigger.

ECHEVERIA
E. candida A very short-stemmed rosette of pointed leaves heavily covered with white meal. Flowers also white.
E. crenulata A loose rosette on short stems with leaves up to a foot long and six inches wide. Wavy leaf edges. Flower stalks to three feet with sparse yellow and red blossoms. Sometimes these plants only make it to the pale green stage. Shop around for a specimen with *thick* white powdering.
E. farinosa A many-branched, low-stemmed plant with narrow, pointed leaves and densely covered with mealy white powder. The yellow flowers are not often produced in captivity.

PACHYPHYTUM

This thick *(pachys)* plant *(phytos)* from Mexico was once classified with the *Cotyledon* genus, and is closely related to the echeverias—close enough to hybridize. Although they are similar to the echeverias, the rosette form is more open and the leaves much thicker. Their culture, however, is the same.

P. oviferum (Moonstones) A nice little plant with fleshy round leaves, dusted with fine white powder. It looks like a loose arrangement of sugar-coated candies. Flowers are pendant from a slender stalk and reddish in color.

POT CULTURE Keep water and hands off the leaves. Otherwise their culture is the same as it is for others of their genus already discussed on previous pages.

fringed flowers

The stems of the members of the *Stapelia* genus are nude, but some of these succulents have hairy flowers. The genus was named by Linnaeus for Johannes van Stapel, a medical doctor from Amsterdam. There are some 80 to 100 species of this African succulent with the four-sided stems and the funny flowers. Funny as in: The five-pointed, starlike blooms with fringed edges come in sinister colors with strange, mottled patterns. Funny as in: Some of the flowers get to be a foot and a half across. And not funny as in: Many stapelias have an odor that would fell an ox at close range. Popular common names: Starfish flower and Carrion flower.

The plants themselves range anywhere from a few inches high to nearly three feet, but basically they look alike: succulent, four-cornered stems with tubercled bumps along the edges. (Africans regard these fingerlike stems as quite a delicacy.) All of the stapelias are easy to grow and bloom quite freely. Don't let the odor of the flowers stop you from trying these plants; it's not offensive unless you get very close and breathe deeply. And then, too, *Stapelia variegata* and its hybrids are unscented, as are several other species. The same cannot be said for the furry-flowered ones that are discussed here.

S. Desmetiana A beauty, with foot high, velvety stems and large flowers colored pale to dark purple. Long white hair fringes the edges and center of each wrinkly flower.

S. gigantea Nine-inch stems and huge flowers (12 to 16 inches) that are purplish brown, yellow mottled and fringed around the edges.

S. grandiflora A spreading clump of stems growing to about a foot high. Flower stems form at the base of the new shoots and bear wrinkled, purplish, striped blooms covered with fine, soft gray hairs. Flowers to six inches across.

POT CULTURE Stapelias like a heavier soil with more humus than most succulents and full sun or partial shade. Protect them from the scorching sun during the hottest days of summer. Standard wet-dry-wet watering in summer; less in winter. Stems should be plump and full; if they start to get limp looking, water more frequently. Propagate from shoots; they root easily. Seeds germinate very fast, some as rapidly as 24 hours. Seedling roots are very tender, so be careful when transplanting. Time from seed to flowering size is about three years.

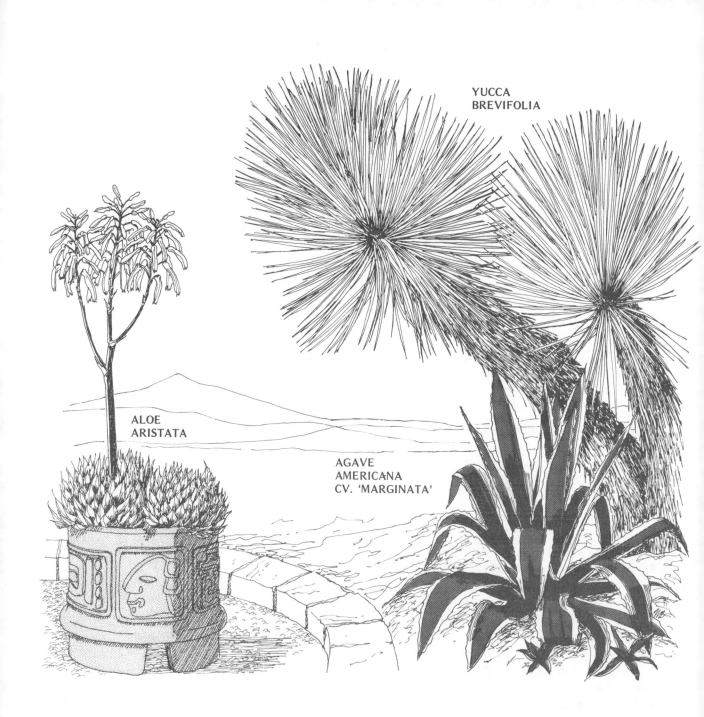

YUCCA
BREVIFOLIA

ALOE
ARISTATA

AGAVE
AMERICANA
CV. 'MARGINATA'

the tolerant classics:
the rosette form

Some plants grow in rosettes, a classic form in nature and one much copied by man. For centuries the rosette design has been used on everything from buildings to embroideries. Botanical rosettes come in several styles: some large, loose and not too organized; some small, tight and very precise. Succulents, of one genus or another, manage to hit all style categories—sedum, aeonium, echeveria, for instance. And, the following tolerant six.

These six tolerant classics demand their own section; they are easy to grow but consider themselves too unique to associate with the common herd. One of them is a cactus, five of them are not. The cactus deserves an "E" for effort, though. It doesn't look like the rest of its family.

For purposes of the most primitive sort of organization, the six tolerant classics can be divided into the following categories:

The Big Three: *Agave, Aloe* and *Yucca.*

The Small Two: *Haworthia* and *Gasteria,* both classified with the aloes at one time.

One Pretender: *Ariocarpus,* a cactus that sneaks around disguised as a short, fat aloe.

the big three

Agave, Aloe and Yucca are big and bold, except for the dwarf forms, and they grow quite vigorously into space-taking plants. They are spectacular additions to a room, if you can accommodate them. Unlike many succulents who do not take kindly to any kind of fertilizer, these three definitely need a shot in the arm of low-nitrogen fertilizer during their growing season.

AGAVE
Agave (agauos: noble) is a genus of some 300 species and is a member of the amaryllis family. It is sometimes known as the American aloe and in Mexico it is called Maguey, which doesn't help any when people are trying to sort them out.

The agave is an important plant. Even Cortés was impressed. While marching through Mexico making conquests, he took time out to wax poetic about the agaves: "Surely, never did nature enclose in so compact a form so many of the elements of human comfort and civilization." He noted too that the Aztecs grew them on plantations as a cultivated crop and that the crushed leaves were made into a fine fabric paper said to be softer and more beautiful than parchment. He also saw that agaves made an impenetrable thatch for dwellings, that the roots were good to eat, that the sharp terminal spines were used for pins and needles and that thread was made from some species. And more than likely he contemplated the translation of the name of the terrible Aztec war god, Huitzilopochtli: the hare of the aloes. (Agaves at this time were still called aloes.) The Aztecs listed over 300 uses for the plant, and while Cortés noticed most of them, he missed the social implications of the henequen species. But then he probably didn't have time to get philosophical.

THE POWERFUL HENEQUENS
To build great stone structures, be they pyramids or temples or palaces, three things are of absolute necessity—stones, men and ropes. And no matter how near the quarry a building is being constructed or how many men you have ready to go to work, without rope the huge stone blocks are immovable. The ancient Egyptian, Mayan, Aztec and Incan societies were builders without equal, but they could never have achieved their political, religious or architectural dreams had it not been for their thick, strong ropes. Rope was a source of power and the advancement of civilization depended on it. In the Americas, agaves were the source of sisal, which was made into ropes generally believed to be superior to the Egyptian date-palm fiber ropes.

The Incas were renowned for their suspension bridges. In their mountainous homeland it was either build bridges or stay home. The supporting ropes were as thick as a man's body and as a rule they lasted much longer. The famous Bridge of San Luis Rey, built around 1350, literally hung in there for well over 500 years.

Besides heaving and hoisting lines, the agave fibers were used for bowstrings, fishing lines, nets and rigging. If it weren't for these wonderful plants, all of the ancient American peoples would have probably just bumbled around in the backwoods trying to find something to use for a pajama cord, forgetting all about building empires—a one-handed civilization.

With the discovery of the fibrous agave, the Incas became men of vision—perhaps too visionary. They also discovered that the central portions of the agave fermented rather well. Mescal, pulque and tequila almost turned them again into a one-handed civilization. It was only the fact that they hadn't invented the swizzle stick that saved them.

The best-advertised agave is the *A. americana* or Century plant, which does not take 100 years to bloom as some would have it. The plant matures and blooms in anywhere from seven to 20 years, allowing for conditions such as weather, soil and location. The flower spikes are spectacularly tall, 20 feet or so, and it is not too surprising that after an effort like that the plant dies of exhaustion. All agaves do have a habit of cashing in their chips after they flower, but as indoor potted plants they seldom put forth flowers and if they do happen to at that stage of maturity there are usually offsets that can be repotted to perpetuate the species.

If you are tired of docile, modest, "ah shucks" plants, you might like to try one of these historically and economically important agaves. But as they are plants of consequence, distinguished and significant, you will have to live with them on their terms. And that means, very carefully! Most of them have very long and piercingly sharp terminal spines. It is suicidal to put them in a heavily trafficked area. The smaller species are easier to manage, but still demand respect.

A. attenuata Not a dwarf, or even very small; up to two-and-a-half foot leaves, but very nice with gray-green coloration and no spines. Will develop a trunk with age. Greenish-yellow flowers on arching spikes. One of the easiest and best for house plant culture.

A. horrida, A. stricta and the miniature *A. Patoni* also are tolerable around the house, although the first two may eventually crowd you out.

A. parviflora A dwarf, thick-leafed species. The leaves are about four inches long and split into threads at the ends, making it look a little unkempt.

A. utahensis var. *nevadensis* This plant looks more like a fright wig than it looks like Utah or Nevada. It has fat, toothed leaves which grow fairly vertically for an agave and end with light-colored spines almost as long as the leaves. A dwarf.

A. Victoriae-Reginae One of the most popular agaves, having thick, dark green leaves with white stripes and three blackish spines on the ends. It grows in a stemless rosette form and reminds me of a pile of boomerangs. After many years it may put forth a flower stalk some 12 feet tall, which could be a problem if you have an eight-foot ceiling. Flowers are greenish white. The plant will get up to a couple of feet across. If you don't have space for it, try the variety *compacta*.

POT CULTURE All agaves are very easy to care for. The soil mix should be very porous. Broken brick, small gravel or coarse sand should be added to a fairly nourishing humus. Agaves like lots of light and sun, and sufficient water during the spring and summer growth period. Feed once or twice during that same period with half-strength low-nitrogen fertilizer. Do not repot too often; they usually can stay put for several years and seem happier if they are not moved. In the winter they appreciate a light, dry and cooler location of 45° to 50° F.

Propagate from seeds if the plant blooms. Offsets are usually more likely though; root in damp sand.

ALOE

Aloes are succulent members of the lily family (from the Greek *aloe* meaning bitterness) and are very much like the American agaves. They are native to Africa and the Mediterranean area, with the southerly types being more succulent than their northern cousins. There are several hundred species and varieties, and a great diversity of form: flat rosettes, shrubs and treelike plants of 30 feet.

The juice in the leaves has been used medicinally for centuries; the Greeks were using it as a potent drug as early as 4 A.D. The gel-like juice was used mostly to heal wounds and burns, although the Orientals used it for embalming purposes and the species *A. socotrina* was given as a laxative.

Unlike the agaves, aloes are not shy about blooming indoors, providing they get their daily allotment of sun. Best suited to cultivation are the small, short species or the dwarfs.

A. arborescens (Tree aloe or Candelabra plant) Branching stems with gray-green, spine-edged leaves; winter flowering, bright red to yellow. Good only when young as a pot plant indoors, unless you have someplace to put a 15-foot, very toothy plant—*very* toothy.

A. aristata Dwarf rosettes, up to a foot high, with thin leaves, lightly toothed and spotted. Orange-red flowers.

A. brevifolia A small plant with three-inch silver-green or gray-green leaves and clusters of red flowers that bloom off and on all year. Also available in a variegated form.

A. haworthioides A dark green, very spiny little plant.

A. nobilis (Golden-tooth aloe) This one is a handsome plant. It has thick, dark green leaves with pale yellowish-green, toothlike bumps scattered all over it and clustered orange-red flowers on a two-foot stalk. Usually blooms in June.

A. nobilis 'Gem' (Gem-tooth aloe) A hybrid with more prominent "teeth," and bell-shaped flowers, yellow to orange.

A. spinosissima A dull, dark green rosette with red flowers and large "teeth."

A. variegata (Tiger aloe or Partridge-breasted aloe) One of the best indoor aloes. Triangular leaves with bands of dark green across them, growing opposite each other. Really more a fan shape than a rosette. Tubular, reddish-pink, green-edged flowers on a tall stem. Propagated from shoots sent up from below soil level.

A. vera This plant is still one of the best all-round healers for burns and scrapes. Many commercial ointments contain its juice, but it's more fun to grow your own. Break off a leaf and apply the jelly-like goop; keep the area moist for a while. Pain will be eased considerably and healing will be promoted. You can wrap the unused piece of the leaf in plastic and put it in the refrigerator until it is needed again. *A. vera* is not one of the most handsome of the genus, but its dark green, toothed leaves make up for it by being a handy medicine cabinet.

POT CULTURE Aloes will tolerate light conditions ranging from partial shade to bright sun, providing you don't try to parboil them during the hottest months. The leaves will get longer in dim light, which is not unattractive, but the plant probably won't bloom. Soil should be very coarse but rich in loam or humus. Liquid fertilizer can be given once or twice in the summer; never in the winter. Water when soil goes dry in the summer and leave dry for short periods in winter; aloes do not like to be damp in winter, and like to be cooler but not cold (minimum of 50° F).

Propagation by offsets or shoots, or seed. Germination of seed is very slow unless the temperature is at least 70° F.

YUCCA

Another genus of the lily family with about 40 species, and native to North America and the West Indies. The plants vary in size and form, from rosette shrubs to trees. They all have white or whitish flowers and some have sharp-tipped, dangerous leaves. Early Spaniards, noting the huge flower-topped stalks, called them "Candles of the Lord." Other Europeans saw the sharp points on the leaves and remembered certain Spanish inclinations, so they called them "Spanish Bayonets." The local Indians, not nearly as lyrical, called them "Soapweed."

The Indians made soap from the roots of some species and although yucca soaps are showing up again as organic beauty products, the plants proved to be more useful than as just a source of shampoo. The tender young shoots were eaten and the seeds ground into a cereal-like mush. (Some species also have an edible purple fruit.) The leaf fibers were made into baskets, ropes and sundry items, including saddle blankets. During droughts, cattle foraged for the species *Yucca elata*.

Yucca is one of the few plants to grow in the gypsum dunes of New Mexico's White Sands Desert, and because of its sturdy root growth it is useful in the control of drifting sand. With prevailing winds and without the yucca, New Mexico might very well have drifted right into Arizona and disappeared. Understandably, the people of New Mexico have named it their State flower.

The flower spike is spectacular: clusters of white blossoms, many varieties with a heady perfume given off at night to attract the moths that pollinate the plant. These moths, *Pronuba yuccasella*, are in fact the only insects interested in pollinating the yucca. No pronuba moths, no yucca. And probably, no yucca, no pronuba moths. These little flutter bugs will lay their eggs nowhere else but in this particular plant. The whole mutual admiration society has gone so far that, as different species of yucca have evolved, so have different species of pronuba moths. Custom-tailored moths yet!

The Joshua tree of the Mohave Desert, *Yucca brevifolia*, is evidently considered to be more than an informal western movie institution because it has an official national status: Joshua Tree National Monument, in California. But if an experiment back in the 1840's had been successful, there wouldn't have been enough Joshua trees left by now to make a National Stump out of. Seems an English company tried using this particular yucca as a paper pulp source. Reports have it that an edition or two of the *London Daily Telegraph* were rolled off the presses on Joshua tree paper, but as the pulp had a tendency to heat up and sour during the sea voyage from America to England, it was not something the company wished to continue doing. Not only was it too expensive, but it was horribly smelly.

Y. elephantipes (Yucca Cane plant) Looks like a giant *Dracaena* with a woody trunk or trunks. A warm-growing species, which does well indoors. It does not have a spiny tip and the tiny teeth on the leaf edges have to be touched to be noticed. In the wild, it can reach more than 30 feet in height; in a pot it can still get too big for its britches, but it is an effective plant if you have room for it. Minimum temperatures are 50° to 55° F.

Y. glauca (Small soapweed) Stemless or nearly so, with leaves one to two feet long and margined with white. Greenish-white flowers.

Y. gloriosa (Soft-tip yucca) Another warm-growing type, with dark green leaves atop a woody trunk. Easy to grow and be around. If you notice black areas on the leaf edges, it may be from overwatering. A variegated form is also available.

Y. recurvifolia or *Y. pendula* Usually a single trunk, but may branch with age. Beautiful green-blue-gray leaves, two to three feet long with a harmless spine at the tip. Spreads by offsets.

If you want to try some of the stouter species, such as *Y. aloifolia, Y. brevifolia* or *Y. Whipplei,* please be careful or you will be stuck, stabbed and diced into bite-size pieces. They have very sharp leaf margins and sharper terminal spines.

POT CULTURE Yuccas are vigorous growers and need a rich heavy soil; add leaf mold or humus generously but don't overlook their need for good drainage. With lots and lots of sun and a coolish (45° to 50° F) winter rest, you may be rewarded with a stalk of flowers. In summer, drench with water, let just dry and drench again; in winter, give less water and a longer dry period but don't forget it entirely.

The *elephantipes, gloriosa, recurvifolia* and *glauca* species are warm growers (minimum 50° F) and will do well with normal household temperatures. The stouter species mentioned like cool temperatures and can be very difficult indoors. In their natural habitat, these species get snowed on, and unless you can arrange to have an occasional light snowfall in your kitchen, they are better left to the great outdoors.

Propagate yuccas from offsets.

the small two

The Small Two are good choices for growers who don't have room for The Big Three, or for those of us who can't count on having the sun blaze through our windows for more than two days in a row. Neither one of them likes bright, direct sun.

HAWORTHIA

A South African member of the lily family, named after an English authority on succulents, Adrian Hardy Haworth. These plants, once considered part of the genus *Aloe,* grow in a rosette form and have two types of leaves: the banded or striped aloe type with sharp points, or the thick, flat-topped kind with "windows," small transparent areas that act as screening devices against the intensity of the sun. Both types are small growing and do very well as house plants. Their flowers are borne on a stem around a foot high, are small, and as far as beauty goes, are nothing to get excited about.

The small, compact species are well suited to dish garden culture, or as singly potted plants. A few of them will eventually cascade, making them good candidates for hanging pots. All of them show some degree of self-discipline and are not likely to get out of control.

H. attenuata Either stemless or very short-stemmed rosettes and dark green leaves heavily marked with raised white tubercles, or "dots." Will spread into clumps. Flowers "blah pink."

H. blackbeardiana A dense, compact, many-leafed rosette with darkened, wispy tips.

H. cymbiformis Stemless and flat with spreading leaves as broad as they are long, pale green with darker green veins on the tips. Very compact and precise. The variety *translucens* is, as the name suggests, nearly translucent.

H. fasciata This plant, or one of its varieties, is the best known of the haworthias. It grows in stemless rosettes of three-inch-long, narrow, dark green leaves which are banded with closely set white dots. The flowers are whitish green. Offsets freely. Compact.

H. Reinwardtii An upright, rosette column of about six inches with short, thick, rough-edged leaves. The varieties *tenuis* and *riebeckensis* will eventually succumb to the force of gravity and become a cascading or hanging form. There are many varieties of this plant, each one differing in type of banding or spotting.

H. setata (Lace haworthia) A stemless rosette of dark green leaves marked with translucent white areas and edged with white, bristly teeth. A small (leaves about an inch long), lacy-looking plant.

H. truncata A small, very succulent plant about two inches in height. It has two rows of thick leaves that are flat on top, as if cut off. These flat tops house the "windows," and in their African home ground, these plants are usually buried in the soil right up to their sunglasses.

H. turgida A small, short-stemmed (blunt-ended and nearly cylindrical) plant with translucent green coloration and paler banding.

POT CULTURE Most are happy in morning sun or bright diffused light. Bright, hot afternoon sun is not really a haworthia's cup of tea. Usually, the species with hardier leaves can take more sun than the tender leafed. If the leaf tips of your plant get dry and brown, give it more shade.

Haworthias usually do their growing in the spring and fall, resting through the summer and again midwinter. When you see signs of growth, keep watered adequately. Slack off when the plant is resting, but don't let it go bone dry for any length of time. The minimum winter temperature is 50° F.

Propagate from offsets or seed.

GASTERIA

Also a South African member of the lily family and similar to the aloe. The generic name refers to the swollen base of the flower tube (*gaster:* belly). A fitting name perhaps, but not too genteel. These are orderly little plants which are generally stemless and grow with their leaves in ranks of two, once in a while as a rosette. The leaves are sturdy and leathery; the plant is very hardy and nearly indestructible.

These succulents are not above a little hankypanky, and will readily hybridize with each other or a haworthia, with the hybrid X *Gasterhaworthia* as a direct result. Growers who are interested in pure seed strains have a merry old time keeping everybody isolated at spring flowering time. With all this fooling around, we can understand the gasteria's need for a short summer resting period.

G. Armstrongii A stack of thick, dark green leaves, rather warty looking and tongue-shaped. (It looks better than it sounds!) The flowers are pink tubes on a stem about a foot or so high.

G. liliputana A tiny little thing with attractive mottled-green leaves.

G. verrucosa A deceptively restrained-looking plant with tufted, dull gray leaves marked with white. In truth, a real carouser with many varieties and hybrids.

X *Gasterhaworthia* 'Royal Highness' A very small rosette of deep green, white-spotted leaves.

POT CULTURE These plants like heavy soil; clay can be added to create the heaviness as long as the mixture remains porous. Gasterias will do very well without direct sun; in fact, they are not fond of it at all. Nor do they like an excessively dry atmosphere. Keep them on the dry side during dormant periods; otherwise, keep fairly well watered. Don't let temperature drop below 50° F in the winter. Propagation is easy from offsets or leaf cuttings. Seed grows readily, if you want to gamble on whether it comes in true. Smaller species are good in a dish garden.

one pretender

ARIOCARPUS

As an imposter, this cactus is great. It is smooth and spineless, and if it weren't for the areole-produced wool, growing in varying amounts according to species, you might think it was a small aloe or agave. The name of the genus is derived from the ovoid shape of the fruit borne on these plants; it is the same shape as the fruit of the whitebeam tree (*aria*, whitebeam, and *carpos*, fruit).

Ariocarpus has a thick, stout root, like a taproot, which makes it necessary to repot the plant more often than most cactus. Lots of people think these plants resemble chunks of rock, their grayish skin often thick and wrinkled. (In the wild, blowing soil collects in the wrinkles and makes these plants look even more rocky.) Unfortunately people tend to treat them like rocks. Not expecting them to do much growing, they don't give them enough water. This non-growing reputation is a fallacy; they are really quite ambitious when well cared for.

Most ariocarpus come from Mexico, with a few from Texas. If hard pressed, they will cough up a few alkaloids.

A. agavoides This one looks like a tiny agave about three inches across. There are puffs of white wool near the center of the plant and the leaves are ribbed. The rose-colored flowers usually appear in the winter.

A. fissuratus Grayish and flat with three furrows to each thick leaf, allowing the plant to expand or contract according to its water supply. Pink flowers.
A. fissuratus var. *Lloydii* A variety of the above, with only slight furrowing.
A. Kotschoubeyanus The hardest to say and the easiest to flower. Very small, about two inches across, and dark green with a woolly furrow. Clustering with age. Flowers from pink to purply red.
A. Kotschoubeyanus var. *albiflorus* and var. *elephantidens* The first is a miniature with white flower; the second is a larger version, but hardly elephant size.
A. retusus A rosette of triangular-shaped leaves in greenish gray; pale pink flowers.
A. trigonus The largest of the genus, a clustering type, although usually a solitary plant in cultivation. It has thick, upright leaves, a woolly top and yellow flowers.

POT CULTURE Small as these plants are, they have been known to burst their pots. Ariocarpus get thick and swollen around the neck. Between this feature and a big root, they can exert a lot of pressure on a pot. Repot when things start to look tight. Half gravel and half potting soil makes a fine planting mixture.

Water freely from spring to early fall for best growth; keep it drier but not gasping through the winter. Give all but new seedlings a sunny location and don't allow temperature to go below 45° F.

Can be propagated by offsets if any appear, or from seed. Seed germinates at about 70° F and grows *very* slowly.

the genus opuntia

Opuntias are a diverse genus ... no, make that a perverse genus. They are the "jointed cactus" and have an interesting history, most of which spells trouble. Oh yes, the Prickly Pear is important enough to be included in Mexico's coat of arms, and it also has an edible fruit. This fruit was probably one of the reasons why it was planted in so many places—which in turn caused some bad things to happen, which we will discuss later. These cactus are not only dangerous to individuals, but can present a danger to a whole country!

The name *Opuntia* comes from a small town in Greece, where cactus-like plants are said to have grown. The genus has over 200 species and the species are divided into three sub-groups according to stem form.

Cylindropuntia cylindrical, jointed and tall.

Playtopuntia joints or sections flattened into pads.

Tephrocactus cylindrical or globular, low growing with one or two joints only.

PLAYTOPUNTIA

This is the type which is best known and is what we first think of when the genus *Opuntia* is mentioned. The species include the Prickly Pears, the Bunny Ears and the Beaver Tails, and they are the most widespread of the cactus family. They are vigorous growers and because cactus people have always had a terrific urge to cart specimens home with them, these species have raised hob with the natural ecology of several countries.

O. Ficus-indica (Indian fig) grows so rampantly in the Mediterranean area that people think of it as a "native." When Spanish explorers saw the Indians using the cactus as a fruit tree, they took the plants home by the dozens. On the dry, Kona side of the island of Hawaii, *O. megacantha* has spread across the volcanic slopes for miles. It was introduced to the island around 1800 and because the climate was so nice and the lava soil so well drained, it grew to heights of 15 feet. Natives soon gave it a Polynesian name, Panini, meaning very unfriendly. Being a naturally practical people, the Hawaiians not only found the fruit good to eat, but they also discovered a way to ferment the fruit juice and render themselves a little refreshment. (The American Indians had known how to do this all along.)

The worst Prickly Pear consequences were suffered in Australia. In 1788, the first opuntia, O. monacantha (known also as O. vulgaris), was brought to the continent, and while it performed rather well it didn't take over the whole countryside. So, in 1893, some idot tried it again. This time it was O. inermis and it was a blazing success. By the 1920's, some 30 to 50 million acres were completely cactused, despite attempts to control growth by burning or poison. The earlier species, O. monacantha, was exterminated by the introduction of the Coccus cacti insect, but the little devils evidently wouldn't touch an O. inermis if they were starving to death. (The Coccus cacti is the insect used to make the red dye, cochineal, which at one time was used to color the red coats of British soldiers. As it took about 70,000 of them to make a pound of coloring matter, I imagine it was quite a relief to the Coccus colony when aniline dyes were invented.)

The Australian government decided they would have to import another bug, and after some research on cactus pests they found a South American moth, Cactoblastic cactorum, who in the caterpillar stage enjoyed munching on O. inermis pads. They proved to be very useful in controlling the rampant cactus, although Australia may now have a moth problem. I was afraid to ask.

Opuntias were, and still are in some areas, an important source of food, once the glochid-covered skin has been removed. The plant is also used for fencing or hedging, and sometimes for cattle fodder. Before the cultivation of a spineless opuntia (a Luther Burbank invention), the spines were burned off before the pads were offered to the herd. Burbank's non-spiny version was too successful; cows mowed through it so fast that the planted areas became bare in short order. And since the opuntia needs fertile soil and an adequate amount of water, it was a bust. If conditions were that good, something with more nourishment could be grown in the same place. Sometimes it just doesn't pay to come up with a good idea.

Among the playtopuntias there are several species that make good pot plants. One of the easiest is O. microdasys, common name Bunny Ears—a most misleading appellation. If you have children in the house don't allow the name to be spoken while they are in hearing range, or they will be tempted to pat those cute little ears. Call it "Killer" and warn the kids to keep their hands off. O. microdasys is spotted with glochids, and within the living memory of mankind no one has ever been stuck by only one glochid. At the lightest touch they come off by the dozens, and they are so small that it takes a dozen before they are visible. You'll know they're in your finger though, even if you can't see them, because they hurt like the very dickens.

In spite of this charming feature, O. microdasys is a very popular house plant, and a very beautiful one at that. It is small, rather shrubby and emerald green, a color that makes the contrasting woolly tufts of glochids stand out most attractively. It looks like the fabric called dotted swiss, and comes with cinnamon, gold or white dots.

The white variety, *albispina,* is the odds-on favorite. It's all you can do not to touch it! The gold and cinnamon kinds may be listed as varieties of *O. microdasys,* or they may be given a species name. Actually, it doesn't matter what the experts want to call them; it is very easy to distinguish one from the other by the colors of the spots.

If you notice any brown or red spots, and there are no bugs present, it could be that the plant is too cold. *O. microdasys* is a warm-blooded Mexican species and it resents being kept too close to a cold window in the winter. Because of its flat padded form, this cactus may lean toward the sunlight. If you notice that it is developing a list, turn the pot around every month or so during the growing season.

Caution! In the repotting and propagating sections there are some hints about the special handling these plants require, and if you have never tangled with an opuntia, they may be helpful.

There are a number of species in addition to *O. microdasys* that will perform well in pots.
O. basilaris (Beaver Tail) Usually low growing and spreading, with a bluish-green skin, lots of glochids and no spines. The pads are narrow at the bottom and wide at the top, giving them the appearance of a beaver's tail. Flowers range from pink to purplish red. It can take lower temperatures than the others in this group.

O. Engelmannii One of the most common types. The pads are very large, nearly round and light green. The spines are pale and a murderous two inches long. Yellow flowers.
O. rufida (Cinnamon cactus) This one has short, semi-round, thick pads that are gray-green (sometimes fairly dark) in color. The glochids are reddish brown and velvety looking, making the plant very attractive from a respectful distance. (You may find this cactus listed as a variety of *O. microdasys.*) Flowers from yellow to orange.

POT CULTURE Like all opuntias, the playtopuntia types like a little root room to grow in, so don't be stingy with the pot. Slightly bigger than is usual for most cactus, please. And as they are faster growers, they also need a richer soil mixture. In summer they can use almost as much water as any other plant. If you notice that some of the pads are starting to shrivel, you are not watering enough. In the winter, water it often enough to keep the pads plump; it can't take as much drying out as the thicker, more compact kinds of cactus.

Propagate from seed or cuttings. All opuntias are usually propagated by rooting a joint or pad, and as they will root right side up, upside down, inside out and crossways, it's no real chore. A piece of an old plant may bloom sooner than a section of a young and immature one. When indoors, these cactus are notoriously shy about blooming, although some of the dwarf species have shown themselves to be a bit more willing.

OPUNTIA TEPHROCACTUS

These plants from South America grow, in the wild, at high altitudes and like most alpine plants they are small and usually spreading in form. They are much hardier than any of the bigger opuntias and can take lower temperatures; however, they need the absolute maximum in sunlight to flower.

Tephrocactus joints are very loosely attached; in fact, they will fall off if you speak loudly to them. In nature, the fallen pieces either root right on the spot, or else one will cling to the fur of some animal until the beast gets tired of packing it around and ditches it. Using this method of hitch-hiking, the cactus can spread over a large area at a fairly good clip.

Plants in this grouping have tiny leaves on the new growth, but if you want to see them you will have to pay attention; they dry up and drop off very soon.

O. diademata Gray-green, short joints with long papery spines. Sometimes difficult to keep this one all in one piece as the joints are very flimsily attached, and it is branching in habit. Of the same type are *O. articulata* and *O. Turpinii.*

O. strobiliformis An odd-looking plant with pine cone-shaped joints. (*Strobile:* marked by scales, as in a pine cone.) It is greenish gray and nearly spineless.

POT CULTURE Even though the chances of flowers on an indoor specimen are zilch, they are interesting to have around. The clustering types do better in a shallow container where they can spread out. Keep the branching, shaky-jointed kinds in a place where they will not be bumped or jarred, and where they will not attach themselves to a child.

They take less water than the flat-pad opuntias, and can be kept drier and cooler in the winter. In the summer, give it all the sunshine you can possibly find.

Propagate by rooting joints. I am told that to successfully germinate the seeds of these opuntias, they should either be exposed to frost or snow after they are sown, or be given a trip to the refrigerator, as this cool treatment reproduces the natural conditions of the plant. Having had no experience with seeding this particular cactus, I don't know if it works or not.

CYLINDROPUNTIA

Some of these plants have leaves on the new growth, and early botanists were fooled into including them in the genus *Pereskia* (the primitive member of the cactus family), but the presence of glochids changed their minds. The leaves may be a few inches long on some species and tiny little things on others, but they do not last long. A few days or weeks, and they will drop off.

With a couple of exceptions, the cactus in this group are anywhere from difficult to impossible to bring into flower as indoor pot plants, but their fascinating structure and form make them worth having even without the flowers.

The common group name for the cylindro-puntias is cholla, a Spanish word meaning "head-shaped," and the tops of these cactus, with their clustered growth, often look like heads. I hesitate to say "human head" because I've never seen a soul who looked like that . . . and I hope I never do! Chollas have vicious spines, and other than the cactus wren and the kangaroo rat, who both live in the protective custody of the cactus, they are left alone by man and beast. That is, any person with more than two brain cells leaves them alone. Cactus growers, on the other hand, find these mean, nasty, devilish plants completely irresistible.

O. Bigelovii (Teddy Bear cactus) The name makes it sound very huggable. Bah! It is the prickliest of all cactus! It looks furry because the straw-colored spines and glochids are so closely set and numerous. Smaller than the Jumping chollas, which follow, with pretty yellow-to-white, lavender-streaked flowers which don't make up for the plant's nasty nature.

O. cylindrica (Emerald-Idol) Much tamer than the other chollas. Branching trunk with long, yellowish spines up to two inches long; however, the spines are sparse and far apart. New growth has pointed, cylindrical leaves.

O. fulgida (Jumping cholla) A tall cactus with a dark, blackish trunk and green-yellow branches. Grotesque and unbelievably spiny. The joints fall off, and cling, at the merest touch. They do not jump, although you will if you ever tangle with one of these sweethearts. The flowers are pink or white, and streaked with lavender.

O. leptocaulis (Pencil cactus) A small cholla, densely branched with slender, pencil-sized joints. Easier to be around than the others, but still very prickly.

O. Salmiana and O. Verschaffeltii Both are easier to bring into bloom than the others. About a foot high, if kept in a pot, with slender branches and non-violent spines. The first one has pale yellow flowers, the second one has red.

Cristate forms are fairly common in the *Cylindropuntia* group: *O. clavarioides* and *O. cylindrica* are the most likely to be afflicted. Grafting seems to up the odds on abnormal growth, but these two are perfectly capable of it in their natural states.

POT CULTURE Strong sun, and lots of it, if you want those spines to stay long and nasty, or if you are trying for flowers. Like the other opuntias, these plants do best in a rich, fast-draining soil. While they are growing they need watering quite frequently; in the winter they can be kept drier, but not totally dry. If the joints start to shrivel, the plant needs water. Of course the chollas are so spiny it's difficult to see what's going on under there, but it's safe to say that they can use a few more winter-time drinks than many of the other desert cactus.

The best way to propagate the cylindropuntias is to collect all the joints that have attached themselves to the skin and clothing of friends and family, and then pull a few more out of the dog's tail. . . . No kidding, these plants demand respect, and if you can't keep them in a child-and-pet-proof place, pass them up. If you like to live dangerously, these cactus can be propagated by rooting the joints, but please wear gloves! Propagation by seed is *very* slow.

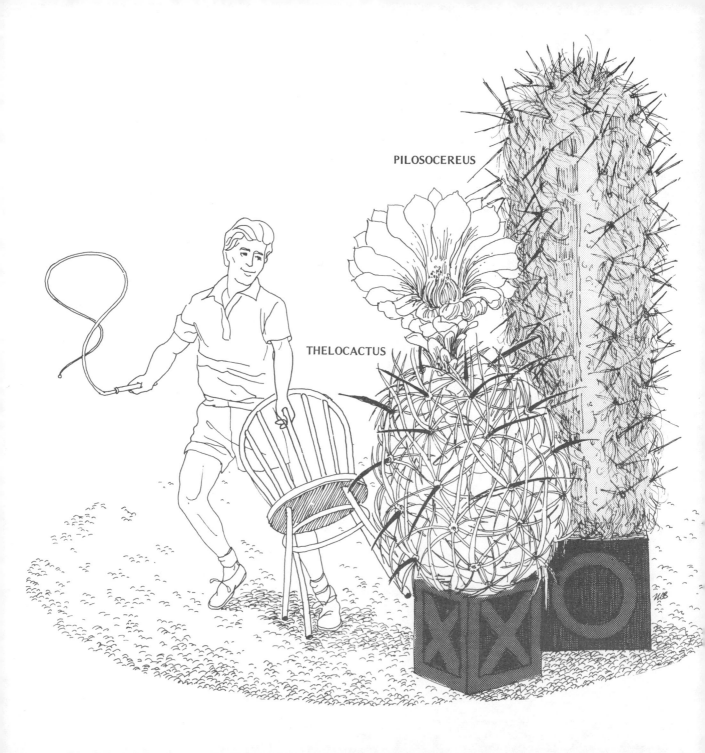

PILOSOCEREUS

THELOCACTUS

the ferocious

A great many people are attracted to treacherously spined cactus. They bring out the beast in some and subdue the beast in others. Some grow them for their effect on other people. This type of plant person doesn't want a "Isn't that a cute little prickly thing!" They would rather have you take one look and bail out the door yelling "Abandon ship!" Everybody to his own kicks.

Some cactus, such as the opuntias, are merely lethal (or close to it). Others, however, are both lethal and *ugly*. They are not for every grower: Some of them take up too much space and some take an owner with a death wish, but they are easy to become firmly attached to, in every sense of the word. Besides that, these truly ferocious plants make very effective burglar alarms.

THE CASE OF THE SLEEPLESS LADY
A family friend, an elderly Victorian-type lady, had lived in a state of constant agitation and sleeplessness since nineteen aught seven, I believe. She always feared that sometime in the middle of the night she would be set upon by footpads or ruffians. For years, friends and relatives tried to reassure her, but she still passed the nights in mortal dread. She had a fixation about two windows which faced a balcony; she was positive her attacker would enter through one of them. (To my knowledge, one of the windows had been cracked open 30 years ago, with the aid of a crowbar. The other had *never* been budged.) I realize that in some cities her apprehensions could be well justified. The last crime committed in her area, however, was when somebody swiped a horse harness from the fire department.

Finally some bright soul noticed that the two windows in question were on the bright, sunny side of the house. Why not fortify them with a few pots of very prickly cactus? I am happy to say that the lady no longer fears the evenings, because laid out under the windows is a mine field of the rowdiest, most ill-bred cactus imaginable.

Although the fear is gone, she still doesn't sleep well. Now she stays awake hoping someone *will* break in. Says she would hate to miss the occasion.

Any cactus in this section is suitable as a protective device, whether permanently deployed or fired as a missle.

ECHINOCACTUS

There was a time when all globe-shaped, prickly cactus were called echinocactus. The old hedgehog mix-up was finally unmixed and the plants were correctly classified and divided among some 28 different genera, leaving about nine species to the *Echinocactus* genus.

To be a genuine member of this mob a cactus has to be barrel shaped, ribbed and heavily spined. It must also be in no hurry to do anything, such as grow or bloom. Flowers form a ring around the top of a mature plant, but as an indoor captive it usually won't do anything that nice. Several species grow white or yellow woolly tops with age.

In 1921, a vast assortment of cactus was shown at an English botanical exhibition known as the Chelsea Show. They had been brought over by the Italians! (I don't know if the United States contributed anything, but I wouldn't be surprised to learn that we had hauled over an Italian plum tree.) After the show, 24 specimens of cactus were presented to the King and Queen as a start for their collection. The King was quite fascinated with the *Echinocactus Grusonii,* and when he found out its common name was Mother-in-Law's Seat, it amused His Majesty very much indeed. Shows you what kind of a sense of humor he had! What the Queen thought about it was not recorded.

E. Grusonii (preferred common name: Golden barrel) A Mexican species, as round as a ball, many ribbed and mantled with straight, sharp, yellow spines. In the wild it can become huge, up to four feet tall and a yard wide, but it usually doesn't reach half that size in cultivation. Mature plants are topped with yellow wool and small yellow flowers. Seeds germinate very easily but it takes about 10 years to get a six-inch plant. Seedlings have tubercles like mammillarias; ribs don't develop for several years.

E. horizonthalonius (Eagle Claws) A flattened globe, much smaller than the others and with fewer rib divisions. Stiff, heavy, grayish spines in vertical rows; pink flowers.

E. ingens A huge beast, to five feet high and wide, with many gray-green ribs and strong spines. Small yellow flowers bloom in woolly top. An easy one to grow.

E. polycephalus A cluster of several rounded heads, growing to a foot across and three feet tall. Flattened spines are anywhere from reddish brown to beige; abundant and long. White, woolly crown and yellow flowers. Likes a pot with a little extra root room.

POT CULTURE The second one and the last one can be difficult; they both like to be warm and free from lingering moisture. The others should present you with no problems if given the usual cactus care—and if gloves are worn when it's time to repot. Flowering chances go up if you can supply sun, and more sun, plus a cool winter rest.

E. polycephalus can be propagated by wrestling off a piece of the cluster. The others can be started from seed, by very patient people.

FEROCACTUS

The spines of the *Ferocactus* are beautifully colored, as well as being very strongly developed (*ferus:* wild). In their native Southwest, they grow to medium and large economy sizes, some species to eight feet or more, and are lumped together under the common name barrel cactus. Smaller plants will often cluster to keep each other company; larger ones are so ferocious they can't even stand each other, and usually grow alone.

Ferocactus are round when young, stretching to cylindrical with age. They are very slow growers with thick, prominent ribs covered with a crop of very formidable spines. Spines can be straight or hooked, or a combination of both. Hooked spines have had their uses, everything from home-grown safety pins to the business end of a fishing line, but what they are best at is snagging people. Use care; their removal is painful.

In their natural desert surroundings, these cactus endure blistering heat and long periods of drought; in cultivation they need very good drainage and cautious watering. Not the easiest to grow, or the most comfortable to live with.

F. acanthodes (Fire Ball or Compass barrel) Both common names are descriptive. Will grow to nine feet in height and three feet across, very slowly. Spines are red, even redder when wet, and the flowers are yellow to orange, bell-shaped and two to three inches across. When not in a pot where it can be turned, the plants often grow faster on the shady side, producing a bulge, and making a handy direction finder.

F. hamatacanthus (Cat Claws) A large plant with twisted ribs and long hooked spines. Flowers are yellow, sometimes with red centers.

F. latispinus (Devil's-Tongue) One of the easier ones to grow. About a foot high, dark green and armed with strong, red, hooked spines; lavender flowers. Its smaller size is typical of all mountain plants; this species is from the highlands of Mexico. Sometimes listed as *F. corniger*.

F. melocactiformis A clustering Mexican plant growing to about two feet. Yellowish curved spines and yellow flowers.

F. rectispinus (Hat-Pin cactus) Spines arranged in 3-D star clusters on each tubercle. Probably the longest spines of any cactus; up to 10 inches.

F. Wislizenii (Candy barrel or Fishhook barrel) Similar to *F. acanthodes* except smaller (to six feet) and spines not as red. Flowers are red with yellow edges or plain yellow. Spines stiff and very thick growing. In the southwestern United States and Mexico, the pulp of the cactus is used to make a very sweet candy.

POT CULTURE For thickest spine development, provide lots and lots of sun; for a healthy plant, careful watering and a very porous soil. A balance between wet and dry periods is sometimes hard to maintain, and the plant will not help you any; it will snarl even when happy.

Clustering species can be propagated from offsets, if you are nervy enough to remove them. Can be grown from seed but it takes years of slow growing to produce a medium-sized monster.

HOMALOCEPHALA TEXENSIS

A round, flat cactus about a foot high and wide at maturity, dark green with pronounced ribs. Doesn't sound too bad so far, but let us continue. Common names: Devil's Head and Texas Horse Crippler. *H. texensis* is the only species, and one is enough! This thing is so solidly covered with stout, sharp, rigid spines that when a horse steps on it, the plant bounces. (So does the horse—about four feet straight up, I would say.) It is very hardy; when it gets through bouncing it will take root and start growing again.

In Texas, New Mexico and Mexico, it grows as a solitary plant out in the open, oblivious to blazing sun, man and animals. Why not? It is almost indestructible.

Newer spines are dark red, older ones fade to gray. The flowers vary between light and deep pink, and are rather feathery looking. Reddish-pink seedpods.

POT CULTURE The most difficult job is getting it into a pot in the first place. After that, your worries are over. Standard cactus care with lots of sun will keep it in good condition. Always use caution when touching this one; those spines are treacherous.

It rarely, if ever, makes offsets. Propagate from seed. I don't think you could make a cutting with a power saw.

MACHAEROCEREUS

Baja California is responsible for this genus of two species. (Some authorities book these species in with *Lemaireocereus.*) They are the nastiest of the nasty, not only to touch but to look at. Although they grow in different forms, both are unusually grotesque. Plenty of space is needed for their culture; the more the better.

M. Eruca (Creeping Devil cactus) A sprawling plant with heavy prostrate stems, and thick, strong radial spines with a long, whitish, dagger-like central. Someone once likened this cactus to a huge, creeping armed caterpillar and it is a very apt description. It does creep forward; the back end slowly dies as new front sections take root. The growing tips are turned up so the plant can go over rocks and other obstacles, like the edge of its container and the sofa. If you can brave it long enough to see them, the nocturnal flowers are cream colored. At least that's what I'm told. Personally, I've never been curious enough about it to stay in a dark room with the creature and find out for myself.

M. gummosus (Mexican name: Agria) An ugly, sinister, upright plant. I should say semi-upright because it still crawls some. It has a very strange form, often tying itself in knots, including overhand, square, half-hitch and double-running sheep shank. Grows to eight feet tall and spreads by sending out a long horizontal shoot which will bend down to the soil and root. After the shoot has rooted it creeps around for a bit, then takes off up through other stems with no regard for direction whatsoever. The flowers are purplish red, followed by an edible fruit. The spines are horrid and pulp from the stem yields a narcotic used to stun fish. Oh yes, it's a very nice plant, indeed!

POT CULTURE Both species will need a large, flat container, one about three feet across—something they can crawl around in. If you can provide the space, and are bold enough to live with either of these plants, you'll find that they are hardy and easy to grow. Sandy soil, sun and moderate watering are about all they will ask for . . . except maybe the southwest wing of your house, including your furniture and slow-moving family members.

Needless to say, cuttings root easily for propagation. Do not handle either plant without gloves; the spines are extremely wicked.

THELOCACTUS

Most of this genus is from Mexico, with a few members from Texas. They are densely spined and small—about the size of a hand grenade, and about as friendly. They have few ribs, which are divided into wide tubercles (*thele,* a nipple). The flowers are large, often quite spectacular, and bloom from young areoles on the top of the plant.

As they can be difficult to bring into flower, there are a couple of species mentioned here which I have never seen in bloom. The experts I consulted didn't agree on color. I'll list the options. Take your pick.

T. bicolor (Glory-of-Texas) Light green, conical and less strongly spined. Each tubercle bears some 10 to 18 long, whitish radial spines with one or more strong, red centrals. Flowers pinkish purple to violet.

T. bicolor var. *tricolor* Densely spined, more variation in color than above. Purplish flowers.

T. lophothele Small clustering plants with a few light-colored radials and one central. The least offensive of this group. Flowers creamy yellow with a red mid-stripe.

T. nidulans (Bird's-nest cactus) Even the most birdbrained of birds wouldn't use this plant as a nest, or build anything that looked like it. The long, long spines stick straight up! (If someone says their *nidulans* is six inches tall, they have four inches of spines and two inches of plant.) The cactus itself is a short conical shape, heavily tubercled and gray-green in color, to about eight inches across. Each areole produces about a dozen stout, long, slightly flattened spines. One report says yellow flowers, the other says rose!

POT CULTURE No special requests; standard culture keeps these plants healthy and bristling, but not necessarily blooming. As this genus flowers from new areoles, giving new growth as much bright sun as possible may spur bud growth.

Large seed germinates well. Offsets from clustering species can be used for propagation.

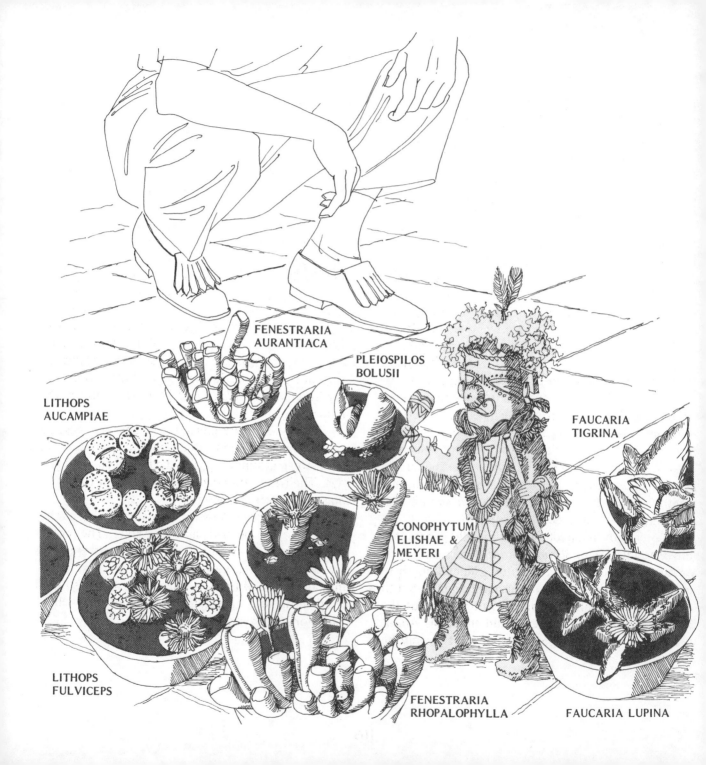

FENESTRARIA
AURANTIACA

PLEIOSPILOS
BOLUSII

LITHOPS
AUCAMPIAE

FAUCARIA
TIGRINA

CONOPHYTUM
ELISHAE &
MEYERI

LITHOPS
FULVICEPS

FENESTRARIA
RHOPALOPHYLLA

FAUCARIA LUPINA

the minis

Why do the tiniest succulents have the longest family name? *Mesembryanthemaceae.* Maybe it helps to keep them from getting lost. Mesembs do love to be lost in a crowd of their own kind and they prefer to grow in dense little clusters, sometimes even piling up on themselves. Because of their size, they evidently feel there is safety in numbers. Mesembs are small, some are very small; you could put two dozen lithops and an equal number of matching pebbles into a container the size of a '54 Chevy hub cap. (It should be noted that an alternate family name is *Aizoaceae,* though it is less frequently used.)

The family is divided into about 20 genera, the most popular being *Conophytum, Faucaria, Fenestraria, Lithops* and *Pleiospilos.* Many of these plants mimic the rocks of their native soil in South Africa; being small and spineless, it was about the only protective device they could think of. And it is a very effective one. Some of them can only be located when in bloom. I have nothing but the highest respect for the discoverers of these plants; they must have covered half of the African landscape on their hands and knees. Noel Coward's song has it wrong. It should go: "Mad dogs and Englishmen, *and plant collectors,* go out in the midday sun."

Some species are green, but many are mottled gray, brown, rust and pink, colors which blend in with stony ground and also help reflect the sun's rays. Their low, rounded shapes are the ultimate in moisture conserving design.

The flowers are large, often twice as big as the plant, narrow petaled and asterlike. The color selection is brief—white or yellow. Seeds are usually enclosed in a capsule which may not open until drenched with rain. Seed can not be squandered in an arid climate; it is released only when conditions are favorable.

CULTURAL HAZARDS

Tiny pebble types thrive in wide, flat containers, usually surrounded by real pebbles of the same coloring and size. Part of the fun of growing them is to match them with stones and watch them disappear. However, it can be dangerous to their health. Mesembs especially hate parties, when both the lights and the guests may be dim. Your pebbly bowl can be mistaken for an ashtray. "How thoughtful," people say. "Such a nice way to do away with smoldering butts." At party time, either warn everybody in advance or remove your garden to a safe place for the duration.

Cats have also been known to mistake these seemingly unoccupied containers for handy litter boxes. If you have just planted a new collection, it might be wise to sit down and have a serious talk with your cat.

GENERAL CULTURE

Mesembs are pretty easy to take care of, once you get the hang of it. They have some unique ideas and a will of their own. Let's start at the bottom and work our way up to the possible problems.

Soil: equal parts sand, sandy loam and leaf mold or peat, with an added half portion of fine gravel.

Containers: well drained and deep enough to accommodate roots. Some species have long roots, in relation to the size of the plant. Clay pots or bonsai containers are best for the plants, and their new owners.

Other requests: Provide full sun in most cases; some afternoon protection if your summers are scorchers. Fresh air and temperatures above 50° F. Water very moderately and carefully during growing season. During dormant periods, provide enough to keep them alive and don't let the roots dry out completely. Don't repot until they elbow each other out of the pot; they like a crowd and it takes years for them to grow one. And *never* apply any fertilizer.

Now, what about those problems? Actually, there are only two and both of them can be easily solved. The first one is the time of the mesembs' growing season. Many of these plants grow in the fall and winter, and rest through the summer. Some do it the other way around. If your plant came without directions (most have them), water it very cautiously until you can determine what's happening. That brings us to the second problem.

If the "what's happening" is *growing*, many of these little plants (lithops especially) will scare their owner right out of his shoes. Their method of producing new growth is very different. New leaves, or bodies, form inside the old ones. When your plant begins to shrivel and develop dry, dead spots, maybe even split down the sides, don't panic. It's growing a new set of leaves! Water is drawn to the new body, leaving the old one to dry and wither away—nature's way of protecting tender, baby growth until it is ready to face the sun.

CONOPHYTUM

These minis resemble the lithops, but with more variety in form. Some are rounded, others nearly heart-shaped; on these species the top slit is shallow and short, like the "eye" in a potato. Several species have two short lobes.

Conophytum (konos, a cone; *phytos,* plant) are clustering, spreading plants, often crowding themselves into little mounds. Their size ranges between a half inch and a whopping four inches.

C. Elishae Two definite lobes, not as squat as species listed below. Yellow flowers. Very similar to *C. tumidum,* which has a short base that splits into two forks. Very unusual looking.

C. Meyeri Light green, heart-shaped with dark green dots scattered over the tops. Whitish-yellow flowers on thick stems.

C. placitum Grayish green and rounded with small indentation on top. Single plant may get to be about three inches high. White flowers.

POT CULTURE General mesemb care. Conophytums dislike being disturbed; don't repot until they are very crowded. Water cautiously while new bodies are forming. Propagate from seed, or break off pieces and root in sand.

FAUCARIA

Toothed, fleshy triangular leaves which grow in rosette form; grayish or gray-green, often with reddish tinges or light spots. Large yellow or white flowers with long, narrow petals. These plants resemble miniature aloes, but are more geometric in form owing to leaves growing in opposite pairs; clustering.

F. lupina Thick mottled leaves with long back-curving teeth like those on a Venus's-flytrap (*lupinus:* wolfish).

F. tigrina (Tiger's-Jaw) Whitish-flecked leaves margined with fine teeth; yellow flowered.

F. tuberculosa (Shark's-Jaw) Very thick leaves dotted with light colored, small tubercles. Fine-pointed teeth on leaf edges really do look like the hungry end of a shark.

POT CULTURE In spite of the beastly names, a toothbursh is not necessary to culture. The requirements are the same as for other mesembs. Grow from seed or a piece taken from a cluster.

FENESTRARIA

These "window" plants are usually buried up to their eyebrows in their natural desert homes. In our homes, where they are not exposed to intense heat and sunlight, they should not be planted deeply. Besides inviting rot, it would be a shame to bury the odd little bodies and miss seeing them; they look like clumps of sea polyps or sponges.

Fenestrarias are slightly club-shaped, cylindrical stems growing in tight clusters. Windows are easily seen; their color and texture is different from the rest of the plant.

F. aurantiaca Light green, glossy-smooth tubes in clusters. Yellow-orange flowers over two inches across.

F. rhopalophylla Pale green clusters about two inches high and to four inches across. Circular tips have dull green windows. Large white flowers on stalks. Usually fall blooming.

POT CULTURE Follow the rules for mesemb care. Propagation from seed; a year and a half to three years from seed to flowering size.

LITHOPS

Unless you can see these plants in the flesh, or at least some color photographs, their beauty will not be fully appreciated. They are often called the "jewels of the plant world" and they deserve the title. There are over 100 of these tiny, subtle gems, beautifully colored and delicately patterned. Don't let the non-green colors worry you. The chlorophyll is down inside the plant and the sun is filtered to it through those markings on top, which are translucent.

Lithops are short, flat-topped and usually smaller than the average gumdrop. Each plant is divided into two sections by a slit across the top, with flowers emerging from the center of the slit.

The common names are many: Pebble plants, Stonefaces, Split Rocks and Living-Stones, to mention a few. The second one is closest to the truth: *lithos*, stone, and *ops*, face.

One caution: If you want a group planting of mixed species, make sure they are all on the same time schedule. It is very difficult to water them properly when some are sleeping and others are making whoopee.

I will list only a very few, to give you an idea of the color variation. In this instance, seeing is believing. Go visit some lithops, in person, if you can.

L. Aucampiae Squat, reddish brown with dark green markings, about one inch wide and not quite as high. Yellow flowers.

L. Aucampiae var. *Koelemanii* Quite round, pinkish and marked with darker squiggles. Its looks remind me of brain cells, but in a nice way, of course. Flowers yellow.

L. Aucampiae var. *kuruman* Also circular in form. An orangy and gray combination of inner and outer colors. Flowers yellow.

L. fulviceps var. *latinea* Whitish gray and spotted with tiny dots of darker gray. Yellow flowers.

L. optica ruba Slit is deep, sections pull apart. New growth is lavender-pink, fading to beige-pink. White flowered.

POT CULTURE Water very sparingly, even during growing season. Keep warm in winter; 50° to 60° F. Grow from seed or section of clump. Handle very carefully; they are fragile.

PLEIOSPILOS

Common name, Living Rocks or Split Rocks. These plants are gray-green or brown-green, rounded forms with darker dots, usually raised. The bodies are split clear to bottom and pairs of next leaves and flowers emerge from the cleft. Large daisy-like flowers, yellow or white. The plants cluster and each plant has one or two pairs of leaves about two or three inches across.

As color variations are very subtle and plant shapes are nearly identical, a description of species would be futile. If you'd like some names, *P. Nelii* and *P. Bolusii* are the most popular.

POT CULTURE A little less fussy and more sturdy than most mesembs, but still highly resentful of lingering moisture. Can be grown from seed or by rooting a pair of leaves from the clump.

the granddaddy of them all

Pereskia is the most primitive member of the *Cactaceae* family and the least succulent cactus. Evidently they had enough sense to stay in the jungle where it was warm and moist, because they retained their leaves—real leaves. They are shrubby or climbing plants with woody stems, spines and large leaves. If you inspect them closely, you'll find that the spines and leaves sprout from areoles, making them a true cactus whether they look like it or not.

The flowers range from white to pale pink and are often sweet smelling, and they are not tube shaped at the base like other cactus flowers. They look a little like a frazzled wild rose. (Although the origins of the cactus family is an unsolved riddle, some botanists believe that the cactus and the rose sprang from a common ancestor.)

Pereskias are warm weather plants, growing from Florida to Mexico and points south, Argentina and Paraguay. Ancient Indians used them for hedges, making them the first cultivated cactus—the first indication of man doing something more useful with cactus than yelling "Yeow!" How do we know they planted the hedges? Well, even though the villages fell to ruin ages ago, the pereskia barriers are still there, as sturdy as ever.

P. aculeata Not only one of the nicest, but one of the easiest to find. This is a large climbing shrub with white, perfumed flowers. If you don't have space, it can be chopped back to a manageable size, but don't try to make a miniature out of it.

P. Bleo and *P. grandiflora* Two more of the erect treelike species. The first has broad stiff leaves and clusters of pinkish flowers; the second is similar except that it has reddish young shoots.

P. Godseffiana Variegated red leaves. It is sometimes listed as a *rubescens* variety of *P. aculeata.*

P. sacharosa An erect shrub which can get quite tall—in the neighborhood of 10 feet—with ideal growing conditions. Pink flowers.

POT CULTURE These plants are not as easy to find as other kinds of cactus, but they are available if you hunt around. Mail-order cactus nurseries usually list them in their catalogs.

Pereskias like plenty of root room, as they are fairly vigorous growers, to 15 feet in their jungle homes. They should be watered generously in the summer, as you would any other house plant, and they should not dry out completely in the winter. Remember, they are the least succulent of the cactus family, and they need water more often.

If they are kept too cool in the winter, below about 45° F, they will lose their leaves. This, however, is a temporary thing and the leaves will be back in the spring. Above 50° to 55° F, they should stay leafed out year-round.

They grow easily from seed and can be propagated from cuttings. Do not callus or dry off the cuttings as with other cactus; plant them right away in a rooting medium. After they have developed roots, pot them in a humusy, gritty soil. Pereskias will bloom indoors, but usually not until the plant is quite large. Give it a bright, filtered-sun location.

THE HALFWAY PERESKIOPSIS
These plants are between the pereskias and the opuntias. They resemble pereskias in that they are shrubs, but they are smaller and have more succulent stems and leaves. The first botanist who saw it probably thought he had a chubby pereskia, but as soon as he touched it and drew back a glochid-covered hand he decided it had to be some kind of opuntia. The *Pereskiopsis* genus is a little bit of both.

In cultivation they take less watering than the pereskia, and a little more sun. *P. velutina* makes an especially good house plant.

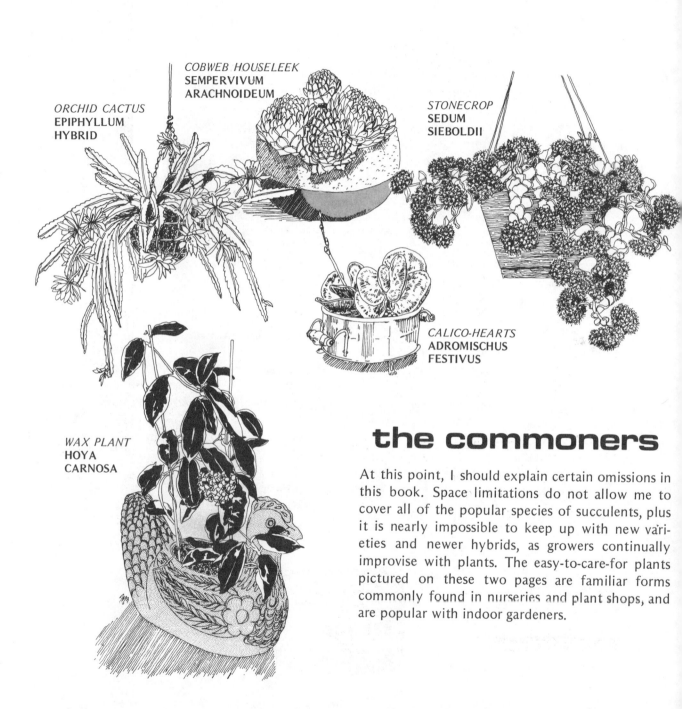

COBWEB HOUSELEEK
**SEMPERVIVUM
ARACHNOIDEUM**

ORCHID CACTUS
**EPIPHYLLUM
HYBRID**

STONECROP
**SEDUM
SIEBOLDII**

CALICO-HEARTS
**ADROMISCHUS
FESTIVUS**

WAX PLANT
**HOYA
CARNOSA**

the commoners

At this point, I should explain certain omissions in this book. Space limitations do not allow me to cover all of the popular species of succulents, plus it is nearly impossible to keep up with new varieties and newer hybrids, as growers continually improvise with plants. The easy-to-care-for plants pictured on these two pages are familiar forms commonly found in nurseries and plant shops, and are popular with indoor gardeners.

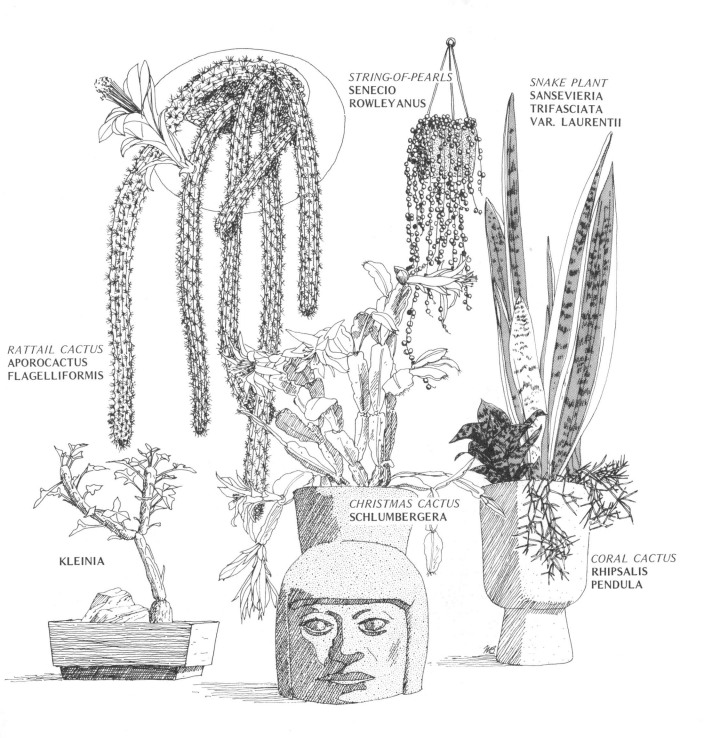

RATTAIL CACTUS
APOROCACTUS
FLAGELLIFORMIS

STRING-OF-PEARLS
SENECIO
ROWLEYANUS

SNAKE PLANT
SANSEVIERIA
TRIFASCIATA
VAR. LAURENTII

KLEINIA

CHRISTMAS CACTUS
SCHLUMBERGERA

CORAL CACTUS
RHIPSALIS
PENDULA

FOUQUIERIA
PURPUSII

JATROPHA
CATHARTICA

the crazies

Plants in this group are usually called "conversation pieces." And they are . . . if you care for that type of conversation. I've found that after the first startled *"yeech!"* most people would just as soon not discuss them at all. Sometimes they would rather not even stay in the same room. These plants have been described as bizarre, weird, far-out, strange and fascinatingly revolting. Quite often the same adjectives may apply to the people who grow them, but then again, many perfectly normal people own one of these monstrosities.

In spite of their unusual forms, the majority of these crazies are easy to grow and about as delicate as a Mack truck. A few of them have peculiar growing habits, so it would be a fine idea to gather all the cultural information you can for your species before you bring it home, or very shortly thereafter.

The bonzai look of some of these offbeat succulents is part of their natural growth pattern, and no complicated rituals are needed to keep them in trim. *Bursera, Pachycormus* and *Fouquieria* specimens have a remarkably effective potential for bonsai that develops naturally as they age. These three are often called Elephant trees, and the fact that they look like a cross between a turnip and a bagpipe thrills some people half to death.

For those who would like to cultivate something *different*, and end some conversations, any plant in this section will fill the bill.

abnormalities

Sometimes a plant's genes get mixed up and it puts out some odd growth. On anything else such foolishness is viewed with distaste and growers, fearing they are stuck with a "lemon," toss it out. In the succulent world, idiocy becomes a valued collector's item. Gives one pause for thought, doesn't it?

CRESTS

Cristate growth is found in nearly every genus; it could happen to one of your little friends. If it does, standing around saying "Well, nothing like that ever happened on *my* side of the family!" won't help; the cactus will do what it has to do. And *when* it has to do it. Deliberately injuring a plant with a knife or karate chop will not produce the urge for distortion.

Crests are low, flattened, intertwined piles of stems. Some people find them attractive; others think they look too snaky and crawly. The following crested cactus are the most common and are sold as grafted plants—wild topknots on a cereus base.

Mammillaria discolor cv. 'Cristata'

M. elongata cv. 'Cristata'

M. Wildii cv. 'Cristata'

Opuntia cylindrica cv. 'Cristata'

O. vestita cv. 'Cristata'

Most crests do not flower as readily as the normal species and the flowers are usually smaller.

MONSTROUS

Cactus from the cereus group are the most likely to form monstrous growth: knobs, lumps, bumps, ruffles and flourishes. Some are dwarfed as well as knobby. One of the most spectacular, and the hardest to come by, is *Lophocereus Schottii* cv. 'Monstrosus,' the Totem Pole cactus. (Description can be found in the Fair-Haired Boys, as the normal *L. Schottii* is white haired.)

Others that can be purchased as ready-made freaks are *Cereus Jamacaru* cv. 'Monstrosus,' *C. peruvianus* cv. 'Monstrosus,' and *Opuntia Tuna* cv. 'Monstrosus.'

SURPRISE!

You may get a potential oddball in a package of cactus seed. The seedling will look normal for a while . . . then, ta-dah! At this stage monstrous plants can be difficult to keep alive, but if they make it they become just as hardy as the next guy.

CULTURE

Both crested and monstrous plants should be given the same care as other members of the same species. If normal growth happens to appear, it can be cut off to preserve the crest.

a bit thick is what they are

When Lewis Carroll wrote *Hunting of the Snark* he made up one of his fine tales of mythical lands and adventures. It was the tale of a globe-trotter and a "thing" which made its home on a far away, desert shore. The name of the "thing" was Boojun. In the early 1920's, a young man named Sykes returned home from the less-than-hospitable midsection of Baja California, and told his father, a botanist, about some weird plants he'd seen. If he had been my son I would have asked him just how long he had been out in the hot sun when these weird plants were discovered. But, the elder Sykes, having great faith, set out to take a look for himself. And found them. And, remembering his literature, said they were the long, lost Boojuns.

And that brings us to the Boojun tree, *Fouquieria Idria columnaris*. (All in favor of the Sykes version, stand up.)

FOUQUIERIA

If the fouquierias didn't have scruffy twigs and a few small leaves, they'd look like large, wrinkled, brown carrots planted upside down! These bizarre Elephant trees are native to areas in Baja California not generally thought of as the garden spots of the world. The climate is terribly hot and painfully dry. Fouquierias store their water in large, swollen, woody trunks. Leaves are produced only after a favorable period, which in their native climate is at least 39 drops of rain.

Flowers, usually red or yellow, are not borne on the branches, but grow on slender stalks at the tip of the plant. Those on-again, off-again leaves and the flower stalks may remind those who are familiar with the southwestern United States desert of another plant. Yes, the Ocotillo is a member of the fouquieria family.

F. fasciculata Very woody-looking, brown-gray base, swollen and heavy. Light green leaves on wizened branches.

F. Idria columnaris Very large in nature; to 60 feet high and 30 inches around at the base. Trunk is pyramidal, very wrinkled and sparsely spiraled, with small, straggly, twig-like branches. Small, fleshy tufts of leaves during the good times. Leaf stems stay on, as spines, after leaves have fallen.

F. Purpusii Similar to the others, but a little more slender based and smaller leafed.

F. Sheveri Body stemlike, but still thick and "bark" covered. Very short, thorny-looking twigs with glossy leaves.

POT CULTURE Well-drained loamy soil with some added peat. Partial shade in hottest summer months and generous amounts of water during growing season; leaves transpire water quickly. Cooler in winter with much less water. Never below 50° F. For best effect, plant in a bonsai container. Propagation is best left to the experts.

BURSERA

This Elephant tree is named for Joachim Burser, who wrote an introduction to natural science in the early 1600's. If something had to be named for the man, it's too bad he was stuck with these bulgy, deformed plants, which look like they are in a constant state of molt.

Burseras are very slow growing "trees" from tropical America, with thick bulbous trunks and a straggling of short twigs. Outer layers of light-colored bark crack or blister and eventually peel off in thin sheets. In their native soil they grow to some 10 or 15 feet tall; in a pot they are a perfect bonsai size.

B. fagaroides Grayish trunk with a thatch of twigs on top. Good bonsai form and very effective, even when leafless.

B. microphylla White-barked trunk topped with twiggy branches bearing very small leaves, in season. Typical tubular yellow flowers on stalks, at the tip of the tree.

B. Simaruba (or *gummifera*) Similar structure to above with darker bark. A source of one type of balsam used as a medicine.

POT CULTURE Same as for the fouquierias. Can be propagated from cuttings; supply bottom heat and put under glass. Not one bursera grower in a million, however, will let you ruin the plant's form by cutting off so much as a leaf. Older specimens can be very expensive, but between 15 and 20 bucks will buy a middle-sized one.

JATROPHA

A turnip-trunked member of the euphorbia family from tropical America (a few grow in Southern California and Florida) with great eye appeal. Although jatrophas have the offensive milky sap common to euphorbias, the name *trophe* means nourishment, and a bitter purgative is made from the plant.

The thick water-storing bulb is evenly rounded and white; some species are quite smooth, while others have brown warty flecks. Light green stems grow straight up out of the very top of the trunk and bear large leaves, often maple-like in shape. They are striking plants, but not gnarled looking.

J. cathartica (or *Berlandieri*) Very round, roughened, white trunk. Light green, maple-like leaves.

J. Curcas (Barbados Nut) Maple-type leaves and yellowish flowers, in clusters. Common name comes from dark red seeds that look like a cross between a nut and an olive.

J. hastata (or *integerrima*) Profuse red flowers with oblong or ovoid leaves.

J. multifida (Coral plant) Rounded leaves with deeply cut lobes. Red flowers bloom in clusters.

POT CULTURE Most species are free flowering; *cathartica* is the freest. Care is easy: porous soil, sunshine and generous waterings when leaves are growing or flowers are forming. Keep drier in winter, but not too cool—55° to 60° F minimum. These tropicals don't know the meaning of the words "frost warning."

a beauty and two beasts

Pachycormus discolor is the beauty of the fat-footed group. It does not look like a lump with leaves; it looks like a very small tree. It also looks like a lot of money when you take a peek at the price tab. The misshapen swelling, characteristic of the plants in this group, stays close to the soil level on the *Pachycormus* and often resembles an exposed root system. The rest of the trunk tapers into a delicate branching pattern, finished off with deeply lobed leaves. A must-see, and probably must-have, for bonsai lovers. Bloom? I really don't know, and everybody I asked was too enchanted with the plant to care. Discolored? The slightly roughened trunk is grayish; nothing to get nasty about though.

This is not a falling-off-a-log-easy plant to grow, but with a little luck and given the same care as its ugly relatives, fouquierias and burseras, you'll get your reward.

The beasts are both in the genus *Cotyledon,* a group that rivals the euphorbias in seeing who can grow more zanies per acre. (Other cotyledons under Fair-Haired Boys: Succulents.)

C. luteosquamata looks like the creature from the Black Lagoon when it's young, and a Martian shrub when older. Clusters of slender fingerlike leaves grow directly from the lumpy, rough, swollen base while the plant is youthful. With age, thick branching stems terminate in the leaf clusters. The base is not only rough, it is cracked and peeling, and dirty looking. (*Luteos* translates to dirty or muddy.) The tapered, curved and cylindrical leaves are a nice shade of light green, if that's any consolation. And it shouldn't be—they'd look like tentacles no matter what color they were. Nurseries should pay us to take one of these plants home! As it is, we have to settle for inexpensive.

Cotyledon reticulata is beyond belief. If ever anything seemed to be a radioactive mutant about to go "beep-beep," this is it. After staring at one of these creatures for five minutes, a little boy I know had only one question: "Is it still breathing?" In all honesty, I could only answer that I hoped not.

A *C. reticulata* looks like an overgrown gray potato with a dozen or so knobs on it, with some thin, bent twigs sticking out of the knobs and a scattering of teardrop-shaped "things" hanging from the wispy top stems. A little net, or a net bag, is what *reticulum* means, in reference, I suppose, to those hairlike stems. Personally, I think it would be a good idea to throw a net over the whole plant and cart it away to a safe place.

POT CULTURE Pot in standard succulent soil with a little extra sand added. Bright light with some sun, or full sun, depending on your climate; they do not appreciate heat prostration. Water when the soil dries during the growing season; less often in winter. Minimum temperatures 50° to 55° F; maximum 80°.

Propagate from seed or cuttings. Cuttings, however, can be tricky and are best left to someone who knows exactly what's what.

it's a perfectly normal condition

Sometimes a cactus is just sitting there, minding its own business, when suddenly and without so much as a "by your leave" it grows a crest. The plant is as surprised as anybody. And some succulents, like the Elephant trees, are shocked when they see how much weight they've put on. But there are others who grow crazy on purpose. Strangeness doesn't come over them unexpectedly; they were born that way, and nobody is going to talk them out of it. Here are a few of these "as happy as if they had good sense" plants.

UEBELMANNIA

Uebelmannia pectinifera A brown cactus from the mountains of Brazil. It grows among the rocks in an area of abundant summer rains, sometimes getting a little mossy around the bottom even though it is very well drained. The plant is evenly and sharply pleated, globular and solitary. It would look quite sincere if it wasn't for the fanciful spines. Down the edge of each pleat, or rib, is a thick row of bristly spines that gives the cactus a neat fringed look. A Japanese lantern with Victorian overtones, and yellow flowers.

U. pectinifera var. *pseudopectinifera* Maybe we should run through that one again: *pectinis*, a comb, and *fera* or *ferus*, meaning wild. So this is a fake wild comb version of a real wild comb! And as it usually works out, the bigger the name the smaller the plant. Smaller and wilder, in this case. This variety is just as sharply and evenly ribbed, as the *pectinifera*, but the spines are longer and fewer. On the original model areoles are not visible through the fringe, on the "fake" they are. Young areoles near the top of the plant are dots of white and at first glance they look like a platoon of mealy bugs in marching formation.

POT CULTURE These cactus need excellent drainage. Water whenever soil dries in spring and summer; keep cool and quite dry in winter. Watering adjustments for these cactus can be difficult, so start out carefully; better too little than too much. Can be grown from seed.

AZTEKIUM RITTERI

This normal one is a flattened blob of a cactus from Mexico, spineless or nearly so, about two inches across. It looks like a taller plant that melted down. The wandering ribs are furrowed and fluted with a V-shaped pattern, and are greenest toward the top. The base color washes out with age. Light pink flowers are borne in a bit of wool at top center.

POT CULTURE Try the usual cactus culture and play it by ear from there; it is often difficult to get established. Water very cautiously until you can see signs of growth, and use a rock mulch. Mature plants will sometimes cluster. Propagation is by seed or offset, and both are risky pastimes.

EUPHORBIAS AND THE LOONEY BIN

The "All Time Ghastly Award" should go to the charmer known as *Euphorbia caput-Medusae*, common name Snake's-Head or Medusa's-Head. It is a branching plant with club-shaped, scaly, grayish stems and a few needle-like leaves. Tiny whitish flowers on the tips of the stems, in clusters, don't make the plant any less repulsive. If the image of a headful of snakes bothers you, pass this one up. It has become quite popular recently in spite of its appearance, and I'm still trying to figure out the social implications.

Euphorbia clavrioides var. *trucata* (Milkbush) has similarly shaped stems, but is lower and thicker, and not quite so revolting. More like mechanized broccoli, only browner.

After those last two, *E. obesa* (sometimes sold under the name *E. meloformis*) is rather soothing: It looks like a baseball, and is easier to relate to. In the sun, the spherical, lightly ribbed body will show reddish-brown stripes; otherwise, it is pale green. If you are interested in growing your own seed you must buy both a male and a female plant. No—someone else will do the intimate checking; they can be ordered in appropriate pairs to save you the embarrassment. With age, it will elongate to about six inches, losing some of its roundness but none of its originality.

The *Euphorbia grandicornis* labors under an all-out, no-holds-barred cactus complex. If anything, it overdoes it; most cactus are not as spiny. It is a vicious, corkscrew type of plant sometimes known as the Cowhorn, with brownish, paired spines up to two inches long. The branching stems are light green with wavy, triangular wings projecting like demented ribs. The plant bears small yellow flowers, which neither the *grandicornis,* or anyone else, seems to get enthused about. Given enough time and encouragement, this colossal faker can grow to about six feet in height.

POT CULTURE   Use a fairly rich, porous soil and give these euphorbias a warm, sunny location. Water when dry, but don't expect them to do well under drought-like conditions; they need a *little* more water than a cactus. During winter give them less water and a warm climate: 55° to 60° F.

E. caput-Medusae and *E. clavrioides* can be propagated by stem cutting or division. *E. grandicornis* cuttings can also be rooted. *E. obesa* from seed only.

For saner euphorbias see The Well-Adjusted: Columnar, and Bushy and Hanging.

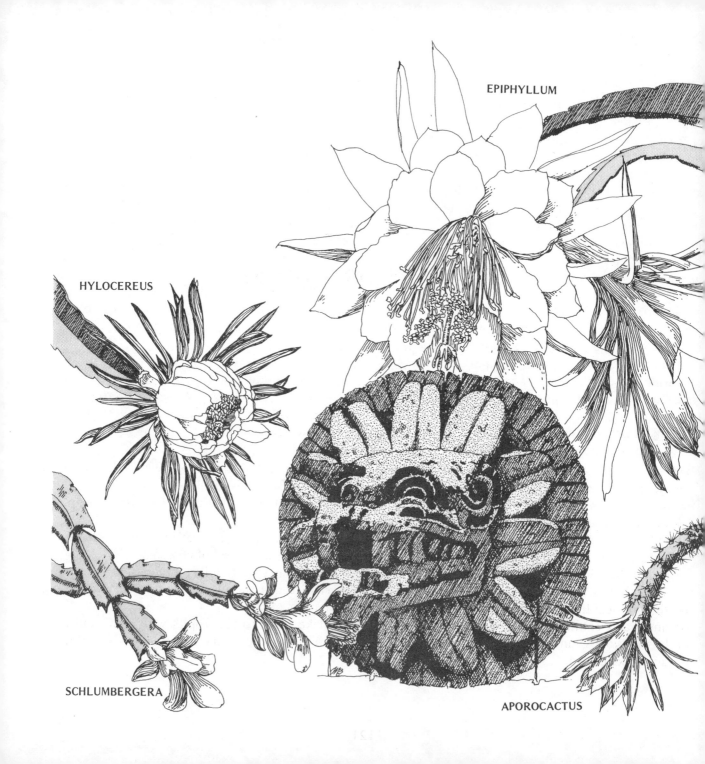

EPIPHYLLUM

HYLOCEREUS

SCHLUMBERGERA

APOROCACTUS

the epiphytes

TROPICAL SWINGERS

Well, no, they don't actually swing from trees, but they do sit up there and sway a little. These jungle cactus from tropical America do not resemble their desert brethern in any way, shape or form, except for two things; they have areoles and they do not like boggy soil.

They grow naturally in forks of trees where small batches of leaves collect and rot into humus, and some have aerial roots which absorb dampness in the air as well. Their root systems are usually small. They have learned that they have only a couple of cupfuls of leaf mold to rummage around in and then ... that's it. In cultivation, their pots should be tight fits; too much root room confuses them and they do not flower well.

An epiphyte's leaves are really stems. They can be flat and leaf-like, cylindrical, jointed, branched or single and continuous. Some sport a few hairy or bristly spines, and some are spineless; a most uncactus-like crowd.

A SOIL MIXTURE FIT TO LIVE IN

It is impossible to reside 10 or 20 feet up in the air, crouched in a tree, and still have wet feet. When these plants come down to pots, they want the same conditions: loose, light, airy, quick-draining soil. And, as their natural medium is leaf humus, they also want an acid soil. There are several ways to provide it and all are good substitutes for their home ground, or home tree.

- Half leaf mold and loam, steer manure, vermiculite and charcoal in equal portions.
- Half soil and half ground fir bark or osmunda fiber.
- Chopped sphagnum peat moss and sandy soil in equal parts, with a tad of charcoal.
- Equal parts sandy soil and humus.
- Half regular succulent mix and half orchid mix, or fern mix.
- Make a trip to the tropics with a tall ladder and collect the humus in the first tree fork you find.

POTTING

Porous clay pots are best because they "breathe," and these plants are used to airing their roots. Crock the containers with broken shards or gravel before adding soil. Use the smallest-size pot the plant will fit into comfortably and leave it there until the pot is about to burst at the seams. The soil can be renewed by scraping off old topsoil and adding a fresh supply. The nutrients will wash down to the roots. .

LIGHT

No direct sun during late spring and summer. Filtered sun or bright light is enough. Weak winter sun is ok, as long as the temperature is cool; between 50° and 60° F, usually. Epiphytic cactus will grow in less than bright light, but to form flower buds they need it.

WATER

Moderately moist while growing and flowering; let soil dry out between waterings, but be there with the watering can when it does. When the plant is resting, water less, but don't let it dry out completely; there are no real droughts in a tropical jungle, at any time of year. Resting time will depend on the species cultivated; usually it's right after they bloom. Some types need a dry period to promote budding, after which regular watering is resumed. This has nothing to do with their dormant season; it's more like scare tactics.

WHAT'S A HOLIDAY?
OR, WHO TURNED OUT THE LIGHTS?

Unfortunately, for them, there are some epiphytes who by nature bloom in the fall, and winter, and spring. Humankind has been boggled into calling them Thanksgiving, Christmas and Easter cactus. No specific date was ever mentioned to them, but by reputation, if they don't burst into bloom at the right time they are branded as radical, anti-establishment malcontents, against society, church and tradition. And their owners are made to feel that they are failures at the green thumb game.

These plants normally bloom *around* one holiday or another. They bloom *exactly* on time for the festivities because they are tricked or forced into it by growers who are out to make a buck. And I don't blame them. The tradition started a long time ago and the general population expects it. I mean, if a nursery owner said, "Sorry, but my Christmas cactus won't be in bloom until the 15th of January," half of the mothers in the United States would go without a flowery gift.

Commercial growers make their preparations in the early fall, one hand on the thermostat, one on the light switch, and the other on a stopwatch. (In this case, three hands is definitely an asset.) Marketable holiday plants are more accurately timed than a NASA rocket launch. If your green friend doesn't perform as well, don't fret or feel inadequate; with a little help and understanding it will come close enough.

These so-called holiday plants bloom according to their natural requirements: cooler temperatures and the right balance of light and dark. They need short days, usually less than 12 hours of light, and temperatures below 65° F, to form buds. Sometimes you can cheat and just keep them cooler, about 45° or 50° F, but for the most part they need natural lighting Some people watch the clock and zip them into dark closets at the proper hour; others put them into a room where bright electric lights, gay parties and late, late movies on TV do not occur. Weather permitting, some growers leave them outside until October and let nature take its course.

To maintain your present life style and still have flowers, try to keep your holiday cactus unsullied by artificial light during the fall and winter, and supply it with cooler temperatures. If you can do this, then slack off on the watering at the same time. When buds appear, give more water and move to a place of honor—not a 75° or 80° F, next-to-the-fireplace spot, but a semi-cool one, or the buds will fall off.

COMMON VS. SCIENTIFIC

Usually botanical names are the best way to identify a specific plant—unwieldy, but definite. In this group, common names are the only things that save us from going totally berserk. To put it rather crudely, the situation here is one big helluva scientific mess!

If you buy a Christmas, Thanksgiving or Easter cactus or a Night-blooming cereus, and it bears a Latin name tag, go ahead and call it by the common name. But, unless you are sure of the odds, don't make book on it.

ONCE MORE . . . FROM THE TOP

The Christmas cactus is often sold as *Zygocactus truncatus*, an old name we seem to be stuck with. The correct name is *Schlumbergera Bridgesii*. (Frederick Schlumberger was an amateur plant person.) Toothed leaf margins are rounded. Flowers are red on the original, but can be white, pink, orange or multicolored on hybrids.

Thanksgiving cactus or Crab cactus is another one often marked as *Zygocactus truncatus*, but really is *Schlumbergera truncata*. Margins are sharply toothed with two large teeth at the ends of the final joint. Usually blooms earlier than *S. Bridgesii*. Orangy-red flowers; varieties in white, pink, salmon and orange.

Easter cactus. Ah hah! This one isn't called a *Zygocactus!* It's usually called *Schlumbergera Gaertneri*. It is in reality, however, a *Rhipsalidopsis Gaetneri*. It looks like a Christmas cactus, but is more upright even though the branches droop on the ends. Red, two- to three-inch flowers in the spring. Many shades of pink and red flowers on varieties.

All three of these plants have varieties which will bloom earlier, and later, and often twice each year. All you can do is give them regular epiphytic care, keep them out of artificial light and hope for the best. They will bloom when they are ready, and without regard for the calendar.

Zygocactus? The name is supposed to be obsolete and nonexistent. It isn't.

The Night-blooming cereus may be called *Selenicereus grandiflorus* or *Hylocereus undatus*. A straggly, climbing, branched plant with pentagonal shoots bearing short spines, turning into flat leaf-like stems. Some stems have aerial roots. Flowers are nocturnal, opening in the late evening and dying before the next day. Don't bother with this one if you are an early-to-bed person; you'll never see it in its glory. And glorious it is! Twelve-inch, heavily perfumed, white flowers open as you watch. It must be pot bound and six to eight years old before flowers appear. *Selenicereus pteranthus* (Princess-of-the-Night) is not as vigorous, but usually blooms sooner; about the fifth year.

Give regular epiphytic care, but don't worry about the hours of light and darkness. It doesn't really care.

RHIPSALIS/HATIORA

Whether these two are the same genus or not is still up for grabs. I imagine somebody has decided for sure, but they are keeping pretty quiet about it. *Rhipsalis* (wickerwork) seems to be the favorite, but *Hatiora* pops up quite often. (I'll bet the 16th-century botanist Thomas Hariot would be pleased as punch to find out that the common name for "his" plants is Drunkard's Dream!)

Whatever they are, these plants grow in bright green, pendulous clumps of slender, jointed stems. The stems are either cylindrical or flat, and very branching. Areoles often bear hair, bristles or wool. Small flowers last about a week.

Plant any one of these South American jungle cactus in a hanging or raised pot, and give it the usual epiphytic culture.

R. Cassutha or *baccifera* (Mistletoe cactus) Cylindrical joints without bristles; forms branches which may dangle to three feet or more. Looks a little like Mistletoe, with its white flowers and berries.

R. cereuscula (Rice or Popcorn cactus) Cylindrical branched stems with tiny, soft, white spines on the ends. Whitish flowers followed by small white berries. This one can take a dry spell better than most rhipsalis.

R. mesembryanthoides A shrubby plant to about a foot high, with upright cylindrical stems and short flat off-branches. Very small spines from fuzzy areoles. Little white flowers on branch tips, followed by pearly berries.

APOROCACTUS

The "almost" epiphytic Rattail cactus from Mexico, *Aporocactus flagelliformis,* will grow up in a tree or down on the ground among the rocks. Slender hanging stems, covered with fine spines, may reach the six-foot mark. Short aerial roots form along some of the stems. Reddish-purple flowers bloom in the early spring.

You won't need to grind up bark chips for this one; sandy soil or a regular cactus mixture will suit it. Give plenty of bright light; some direct sun is tolerated if it's not blistering. Provide generous watering in the summer and don't let the roots get completely dry in the winter.

Propagate by division of the clump or stem cuttings.

HARRISIA

The long slender stems of these plants, with rounded ribs and spines, will need support as they lengthen. They grow to 10 feet in their native West Indies and were named in honor of William Harris, Superintendent of Public Gardens, Jamaica. Sometimes called genus *Eriocereus,* the harrisias are another victim of confused botanical naming. But this confusion doesn't seem to bother them a bit. They keep right on producing large (to 10 inches) nocturnal, white flowers just to spite taxonomists.

By nature, these plants want to grow "up" not "out," but if some means of support isn't provided they are inclined to sprawl all over the furniture. If you would just as soon not have a 10-foot stem draped over an armchair, stake it up or tie it to a hook in the wall.

Epiphytic-type soil is not necessary. A good, rich cactus mixture is encouragement enough. Water as for all of the jungle types and keep warm in the winter, or take it to Jamaica for the season. *H. Bonplandii* and *H. Jusbertii* Both of these species are large growing and very similar to each other: short spined and white flowered.

H. tortuosa This one is smaller, with stems about a yard long. Radial spines and white flowers. Will bloom when young and quite small.

All species of *Harrisia* make good grafting stock. Chop a stem into two- or three-inch lengths, callus off and root as usual.

PROPAGATING EPIPHYTES

Stem cuttings are easy as falling out of a tree; break a section off at any natural joint, let it dry to form a callus, then slip it into a pot of rooting soil. Overcrowded, pot-bound plants can be propagated by division, although they may not bloom until pot bound again.

EPIPHYLLUM

Although commonly called Orchid cactus, *Epiphyllum* means on the leaf. (It should mean: on the stem. The "leaves" are really flattened, scalloped stems.) "On the leaf" refers to the position of the flowers, which bloom along the edges from areoles.

These limber, trailing plants are from the rain forests of Central and South America; they like warmth and moisture and filtered sun. Because of their floppy growing habits, they are either grown in hanging containers or supported on a trellis, and very often they are relegated to an out-of-the-way place when not in bloom. As plants, epiphyllums are not beauty contest material; as flowering plants, they have few rivals.

Hybridizers have had a ball with the epiphyllums, and the dance is far from over; there are about 3,000 named hybrids so far, with more to come. Flowers can be had in any color or combination of colors, except blue, and in any size from two inches across up to about 10.

Here is a very small sampling of epiphyllums, divided into four groups according to the size of the average bloom; they may vary with growing conditions.

Small: two to five inches.

'Ackermannii' One of the originals, and maybe the best known. Flowers early, sometimes off season, with scarlet blooms.

'De Mario' Unusual, white, curled flowers.

'Snowflake' (Cactus Pete) Miniature, basket type. Very profuse white flowers.

'Bridal Shower' Miniature, many rose-pink flowers.

Medium: five to seven inches.

'Adoration' White and pale rose petals, with rose sepals.

'High Hopes' Frilled rose and lavender.

'Feather Queen' Orangy red and purple with frilled edges. Stems rippled.

'Sparkle' Very glossy red petals with many stamens.

Large: seven to nine inches.

'Ceylon' Combination of purples, from lightest to darkest.

'Limehouse' Greenish yellow and white. Beautiful.

'Fifi' Doubled, five rows of petals, in lilac-pink.

'Ruby Snowflake' Profuse, narrow, crinkled, dark red flowers.

Extra Large: nine inches and up.

'Pegasus' Wide petals, red center stripe on purple.

'Moon Goddess' Inner petals all white, outer ones white with yellow tips.

'Bridesmaid' Translucent flowers in shades of light pink.

'Cherokee Chief' Yellow striped, orange petals with light purple in the throat.

POT CULTURE Good bright light or filtered sun for best blooming. Mist or spray during growing season to provide humidity. Fertilize once a month from first signs of spring growth until September, then keep cool and barely moist for winter rest. Protect from freezing; 40° to 50° F minimum. These plants should be pot bound; if their toes aren't cramped they won't flower well. Repot only when container is in danger of exploding.

III CULTURE

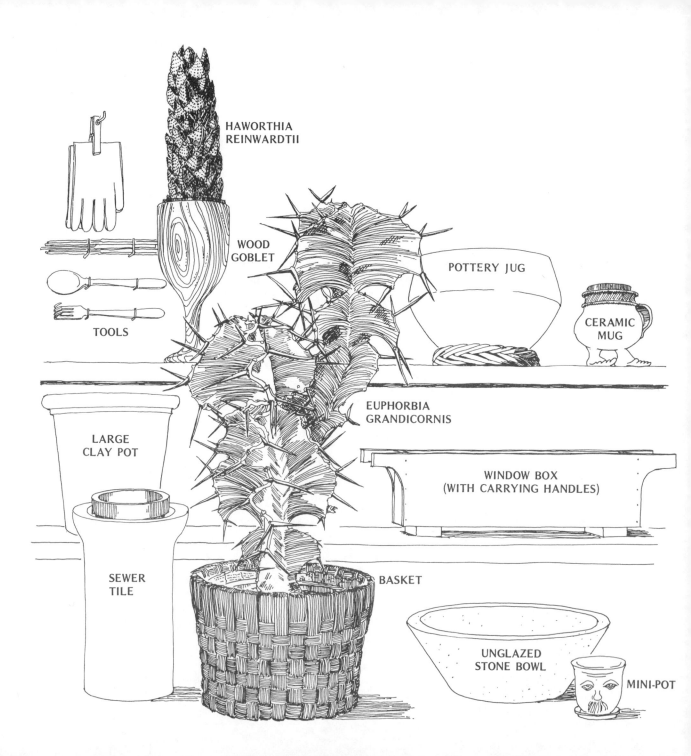

HAWORTHIA
REINWARDTII

WOOD
GOBLET

TOOLS

POTTERY JUG

CERAMIC
MUG

LARGE
CLAY POT

EUPHORBIA
GRANDICORNIS

WINDOW BOX
(WITH CARRYING HANDLES)

SEWER
TILE

BASKET

UNGLAZED
STONE BOWL

MINI-POT

from the bottom of the pot up

Beware of anyone who tries to convince you that there is only *one correct* way to do it . . . and by "it" I mean anything and everything having to do with succulent culture. Certainly there are preferred methods, based on the natural needs of the plants, but lots of succulents are quite willing to adapt to something a little different. A *little* different! They made it this far by being tremendously adaptable, but please remember that it took thousands of years for the changes to take place. You aren't going to change them overnight. Don't try putting a desert cactus into a humid, boggy, enclosed terrarium and expect it to figure out what it's supposed to do to stay alive. It won't.

DON'T JUST STAND THERE . . . ASK!
If you are just starting out into the cactus/succulent wilderness and are having heebie-jeebies about it, don't be afraid to ask questions. Find a sympathetic soul—a plant shop person, a nursery employee, a neighbor or a friend—somebody who has a healthy collection and is able to maintain it. Then ask your questions. Some of the answers may vary from person to person, but only superficially. The basics will be the same.

Once in a while you will get an "Oh, I don't do anything special" answer from a successful grower. Every green thumber does something special, though, whether they realize it or not. Mostly they just care about their plants. Sometimes it's possible to learn more with your eyes than with your ears. Watch a true plant lover among his/her pots and you'll find out what I mean.

Of course, there are times when you simply have to have a more complete answer. My own favorite "askee" is a local nursery owner, and I've been pestering him for quite a long time. Having no illusions about my mental capacities, I just wandered into his establishment one day and blurted it out: "Are you ready for the dumb question of the week?" Luckily he was, and I have been going back ever since. I am happy to say that I have now progressed to "the dumb question of the month." He says he misses me.

Visit the library. Ask questions. Stop, look and listen. Successful plant culture is like kissing: The more you put into it the better the results!

WANTED: A ROOM TO SHARE

Where to put an extra house plant or two (or 10) is no problem for true plant lovers. They have been known to stash the Steinway in the fruit cellar because it was blocking a great southern exposure. Most of us would rather have our plants live with us, instead of the other way around, and succulents will quite happily fit in with any decor, life style, or whatever amount of space is available. All you have to do is pick the right plants for the right places. There is some type of succulent for every location and occasion. They will cozy up to log cabins, to mod or early Salvation Army furnishings, or to Victorian drawing rooms and Colonial kitchens. They don't mind a one-room-with-bath-down-the-hall or a glass and chrome office.

A covey of cactus in a dish garden or a row of compact succulents on the sill take up very little space and in an understated way they will add much to a room.

On the other hand, flamboyant, bizarre, huge succulents can completely dominate a room. The more stark the decor, the more dramatic the impact, and no plant can stand alone like one of these plants can.

It depends on how you want it. Have a mixture if you like . . . it's your house! There are only a couple of places where the presence of these plants may not be appreciated.

COME LIVE WITH ME . . . BUT . . .

Not in the bedroom! Not even if your bedroom has the brightest sun and the driest air. For the most part, when people are in their bedrooms they are not as alert as they might be. There is just too much fumbling around in a bedroom, and most of it goes on in the dark—innocent things like hunting for eyeglasses, bathrobes and light switches, for things on dresser tops and nightstands. High windowsills are not necessarily safe either. There are curtain cords to be pulled, shades to be drawn and let up, closed windows to be opened and open windows to be closed—usually in the middle of the night. So, unless your bedroom has as much leg room as the Taj Mahal, keep the plants in there leafy, lush, and above all, soft!

And not in the bathroom! There is too much humidity, and not enough sun. If you must have somebody to keep you company, there are dozens of pliant tropicals who would be very happy to share your bath.

FLORA VS. FAUNA

Wild animals and native cactus have a healthy respect for each other, especially on the part of the animals. Some goats and llamas get a little "devil may care" about their diets, but the peccary (wild pig) is about the only large animal who will chomp through anything—whole Prickly Pears, spines and all. Besides being blind as a bat, the peccary must be blessed with solid bronze innards.

House pets will usually leave a cactus alone, too, by instinct. Some cats will try their teeth on other succulents, though. Mine had an aloe addiction. He didn't eat the plant, he just seemed to be fascinated with the popping noise his teeth made breaking through the smooth, thick leaves. Even the dumbest cat knows, however, that the chalk-dusted species would be about as tasty as a mouthful of used blackboard erasers, and very bitter ones, at that. Both the texture and the flavor are effective defense weapons against animals, both wild and tame.

The only real trouble between cat and cactus is something called squatters' rights: They may both covet the same sunny window. Cats have no sense of humor when it comes to the territorial imperative, so do everyone a favor and leave a spot open for sunbathing.

KALANCHOE
BEHARENSIS

containers

Small succulents, and some big ones, are sold in plastic pots. Please think of these pots as temporary homes and transplant the purchase as soon as possible. Being non-porous, plastic holds moisture in the soil too long for succulents. Plastic is also very lightweight, and water-filled succulents, often heavy for their size, can make the whole arrangement top-heavy.

Please note! If a cactus pot teeters and falls, *don't* grab for it! This is no time to demonstrate your lightening reflexes. Let it fall. Chances are no great damage will be done to the plant, unless it's a tall, wildly branched affair that should have been put in a solid position in the first place. If the falling object is an opuntia, back off so it doesn't rattle around between your ankles. As rewarding experiences go, peeling an opuntia pad off your instep isn't even a qualifier. Pick up any broken joints or pads with a folded piece of paper or gloves and vacuum the floor. If this sounds like I'm being too fastidious, then don't vacuum, but don't say I didn't warn you when you and your bare feet decide to take a stroll past the scene of the crime.

So, for succulents, plastic pots are usually unsatisfactory on all counts. Clay, terra-cotta, unglazed ceramic, volcanic pumice or lava containers are, however, perfect for cactus/succulent culture. Bonsai pots are also great! Because of the superb drainage necessary to the culture of the mini-trees, bonsai pots have oversized drainage holes. Some are shallow and therefore accommodating to succulent root systems; others are narrow and deep, and completely satisfactory for the bulbous-rooted species. These pots have solid, non-tippy bases because they were designed with top-heavy occupants in mind. And the typical earth-tone coloring is a good complement to succulents. The price for these pots varies greatly, according to size and workmanship, but you won't have to take out a second mortgage unless you go completely out of your mind. Luckily, most succulent plants are quite happy in a small pot.

IN THE MIDST OF IT

If you are potting up a single specimen in a round pot, you will want to position it so it's right smack in the middle of the pot with an even ring of soil or rock mulch showing around the edges. A lopsided arrangement not only cramps a plant's style, it cramps the roots.

Large, flat, shallow containers are usually planted with a balanced combination of plants, a feat which is nearly impossible if you have an even number of plants to work with. No matter how four cactus are arranged in a single planting, they always end up looking like they are standing guard duty. Use three, five or seven plants in your dish garden, and enjoy the results.

Sometimes a snazzy cactus or an exotic succulent is planted bonsai-style in an oval or oblong container. The planting can be very effective if you keep a couple of things in mind. Don't place the plant in the middle. Put it about two thirds of the way across the pot, with the lowest branching

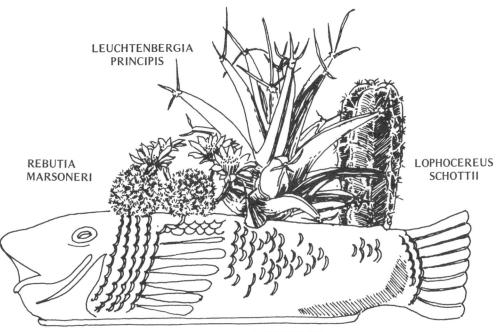

LEUCHTENBERGIA
PRINCIPIS

REBUTIA
MARSONERI

LOPHOCEREUS
SCHOTTII

GROUP PLANTS TOGETHER

stem, if any, towards the center. If the plant has a natural curve or slant, it should face the middle of the pot. If you put it the other way around, it will give the impression that it is about to climb out and walk away. A tall, unbranched cactus can be given this same type of bonsai look, and if the open, empty side of the pot upsets you, an angular rock, judiciously placed, may be used. Once you get used to thinking of open space as a balancing entity in itself, however, the rock may prove to be superfluous.

Sometimes small figurines can be used effectively in cactus dish gardens. Other times they are just plain awful. The best gardens usually incorporate a small animal nestled among the plants in a natural manner, and in a natural color. I don't care

how cute that lavender bunny with the green eyes is; keep him on the shelf and find a dull-glazed brown one in the proper scale to tuck near to your cactus. When using accessories of any kind, always think in terms of what would be there naturally. And don't move in a population explosion. One tiny mouse at the base of a group of barrel cactus is an asset; the entire family can be a liability.

The exception to this restraint with accessories is a child's garden. If your children want their own cactus garden, and most of them are fascinated with them, let him and/or her add whatever extras they want to, even if it's a toy Sherman tank or a garishly painted troll. If something makes a plant garden a special, private thing for a child, leave it.

WHO SAID IT HAD TO BE
A REGULATION POT?

Natural materials, such as seashells, hollowed-out lava rocks, chunks of wood and logs, can be effectively used as containers for succulents. Shells should have a couple of holes drilled in the bottom for drainage, but wood and porous lava are perfect left as is.

If you want to plant in or on pieces of driftwood from the seashore (and there are some magnificent ones), soak the wood in fresh water for a few days to leach out the salt. Pack some soil into a natural crack or hollow, or chip out a spot and plant your succulents. The kinds that stay reasonably flat and spreading usually look best. Of course the wood will eventually rot out and crumble all over the floor, but it takes a long, long time for that to happen.

One of the most spectacular outdoor "containers" I ever saw was the shingled roof of a root cellar. It was more than half-covered with masses of assorted sedums. The lady who owned it knew that in a few years her rotted roof would be right down around her roots, but in the meantime she thought the display was worth it. I wholeheartedly agreed, but then I wasn't going to be paying for new shingles either.

THE SAUCER TRICK

The old-fashioned red saucers made to go under standard clay pots are very good as succulent planting containers. They come in all sizes, suitable for single specimens or group plantings, and they are inexpensive. They will need, however, to have drainage holes drilled in the bottom, but the job requires no great feats of skill. A small hand drill

and a ceramic bit, both available at a hardware store at a reasonable price, will do the trick.

As the drilling area should be kept wet while you are working on it, the best place to tackle the job is either outside the house or in the kitchen sink. I usually end up at the sink. I remove the strainer and place the saucer right over the drain hole. Then I turn the faucet on to a fast drip and start drilling. By putting the saucer over the drain hole, you eliminate the possibility of drilling holes in your countertop.

A small saucer will only need one hole, but from six inches on up, it should have two or more.

POT SIZE

Most succulents like a relatively small pot, one they can just comfortably fit into with a little knee room to spare. The few with bulbous roots can take a larger pot, but not much larger. Never over-pot a succulent! A large pot tends to encourage root rot by keeping too great a volume of damp soil in contact with the roots. In other words, a big pot full of soil stays wet too blasted long.

Round, ball-type cactus are happy in a pot that is about two inches wider than the plant. Tall ones? A pot about half as wide as the height of the plant. Although these are loose measurements and they can be fudged on, it pays to stay close to these ratios.

A beginner's cactus collection usually consists of little plants in little pots. Mini-pots are very hard to regulate; the soil can go from soaking wet to bone dry in a matter of hours and it takes a lot of attention to keep things on an even keel of neither too wet nor too dry. Cactus do not like lingering moisture, but the moisture does have to be around long enough to do some good. Tiny plants are better off planted as a group in a shallow container, like bonsai pots or clay saucers. Why shallow? Same reason as why you should avoid pots that are too big: to cut down on the volume of damp soil around the roots.

As you may have gathered by now, the whole idea of succulent culture revolves around good drainage. Pots, crocks and soil are aimed towards this function, and when the excess water comes out, it's got to go someplace. Some type of under-saucer is mandatory, one that is glazed at least on one side. Unglazed pottery lets moisture soak right on through.

I usually go to the local Goodwill store and buy saucers, plates and platters (great for oval containers) to put under my plant pots. They are ridiculously cheap and the assortment available is usually quite large. Hunt through the stacks for dishes with an "earthy" look; they seem to blend with succulent plants the best.

And please empty the saucers of any excess water; succulents do not like wet feet. If it seems like a lot of trouble, you can learn, after a few waterings, just about how much the pot will take and there will be very little, if any, water to dump. Don't be stingy though, just to save yourself some time. These plants need to be well watered, not teased along with small sips.

HANGING POTS

Many of the epiphytic cactus and some of the trailing desert succulents show off to their best advantage in hanging pots. The only disadvantage is that hanging pots tend to dribble, and gritty succulent soil dribbles a lot. An attached saucer is a

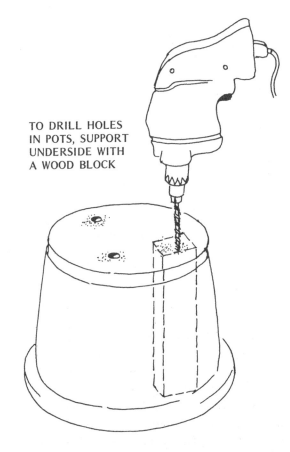

TO DRILL HOLES IN POTS, SUPPORT UNDERSIDE WITH A WOOD BLOCK

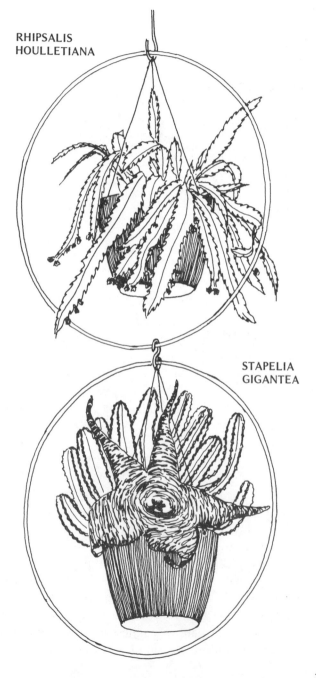

RHIPSALIS
HOULLETIANA

STAPELIA
GIGANTEA

must, unless you can place another potted plant directly underneath to catch the drips.

A few words of caution about putting up the hook or bracket that will support your hanging pot: Plant-plus-pot-plus-soil-plus-water is heavier than you might think. The supporting apparatus had better be solidly anchored or the whole thing will come down with a thundering crash, possibly interrupting a tender moment.

Hooks or screws must go into solid wood, and the ones that come with some brackets are too short and will only penetrate as far as the plasterboard or paneling. This is far from an ideal situation, so check out the length of the screws before you do anything else. And don't even think about using nails, unless they look like railroad spikes and the pot you intend to hang is thimble size.

Of course if you have a brick or cinder-block wall there is no problem. Put your hook wherever you want to. With regular hollow-wall construction, the first thing you will have to do is find out where the studs are hiding behind the paint, paper or paneling. There are several standard ways to locate studs. They are all equally ineffective.

Some people can find stud centers by locating the nails used to hold the covering material on. They use a magnet tied onto a thread, dangling it up and down against the wall until it sticks to the head of a nail. Other people get good results by tapping lightly on the wall with a hammer or their fist. They say it sounds hollow between the studs and solid when on top of one. Evidently they have an excellent ear which I lack. However, I've found that if you tap hard enough you can put your arm into the resulting hole and feel around for the stud. Probably the only sure method for finding it.

Fortunately, most hanging pots are situated in front of a window and this does make it easier. The wall area above a window or sliding glass doors is a solid piece of wood, extending from window to ceiling. You can safely use any of this space, without measurements, tapping or magnetic search.

Some hanging pots come directly down from the ceiling and the ways to find the overhead beams are the same as for wall studs. Risky!

CROCKING

You have the perfect pot. Now what? Before soil and plant are added, that pot needs to be crocked! This does not mean you have to break out the good vintage stuff, it means that something has to be placed over the hole, or holes, in the bottom of the pot. This will insure good drainage and lessen the possibility of having the soil wash out to form a little delta on your table top.

Cactus culturists used to recommend that the bottom third of the pot be crocking material. It's not necessary to get that carried away, but it is a good practice to add a little more crocking than you would for other types of plants (especially if you think you might water too often).

The most commonly used material is broken pot shards, although pieces of Spode tea cups, Grecian urns or dime-store pottery can be used. Don't use a layer of perlite, vermiculite or broken gingersnaps, or any other moisture-holding substance. The idea here is not to hold excess moisture, but to get rid of it.

Save your broken pots and kitchen crockery, or prevail on some fumble-fingered friends, because if you go into succulent culture to any degree you'll need plenty of bits and pieces.

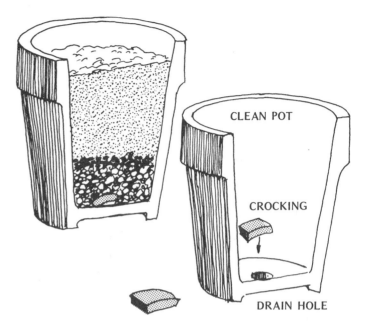

CLEAN POT

CROCKING

DRAIN HOLE

I find that breaking big pieces into little ones is quite therapeutic. I file potential crocking material away until I am in a tooth-gnashing, wall-climbing mood. Then I put the material into a cardboard box and cover it with burlap, newspaper, or whatever is handy, and relieve my frustrations by hammering like crazy.

Instead of the traditional "one piece cupped over the hole," cover the bottom of the pot with shards. The initial drainage hole piece, not to be neglected, should be a good-sized chunk; the others smaller, about fingernail size.

There are some growers who advocate using a king-size piece of crocking material over the hole—as big as will fit into the bottom of the pot. They maintain that at repotting time they can shove a stick into the outside of the hole and push the shard and root ball up painlessly and without root damage. Could be a good idea at that. Experiment.

soil

AT HOME, ON THE RANGE

Desert soil is not as sandy as some people think it is, at least not on the surface where it's important. A layer of humus, thin though it may be, is necessary for the perpetuation of the species. Where does the humus come from? Well, if you start with a little scruffy grass, add a few bird and animal droppings, toss in some small plants that didn't make it, a twig, a mouse skeleton and a couple of bird feathers, some termite mud and a random selection of dead insects, and wait a while, you'll get a bit of humus. Not much though.

A layer of humus is a delicate thing, and it is easily disturbed or destroyed. Overgrazing of livestock, highways, housing developments, dune buggies, jeeps and motorbikes, and fire have all taken their toll of this protective covering. And the new generations of cactus seedlings are suffering for it.

Cactus babies need shade; without it their small, immature root systems wouldn't be able to cope. The parent plant, a bush or even some grass will provide enough shade to give a seedling a fighting chance.

AT HOME, IN A POT

People who wouldn't dream of potting anything in straight sand, not even other succulents, get a Sahara complex when it comes to desert cactus. They should remember that there are no cactus growing in the Sahara!

Cactus can't, don't and won't grow in pure sand! Every once in a while somebody says to me,

"You said cactus were easy to grow. Well, I've been doing everything right—sun, water, the works. So how come they still don't look good?" Usually the problem is very easy to spot, and I try to be most diplomatic about mentioning it. "Listen, I've seen better looking soil in a hotel-lobby ashtray."

Soil is not just something to keep a plant from falling into the bottom of the pot. It has to have some nutritional value or the plant will starve to death. Some plants are gluttons and some aren't; even those, like the cactus, who aren't, need something to snack on. Nutrients are either supplied by the soil itself or by applications of fertilizer. Scheduled feedings take time and fussing, so it is easier to provide a proper diet by using a good growing medium. We are, after all, supposed to be raising cactus because they do not require fussing over. They are also not crazy about fertilizer.

Pure sand, peat moss, perlite and vermiculite used in combinations are called soilless mixtures, and while they work for some types of plants and are excellent for germination purposes, they are not suitable for cactus/succulent culture. As far as nutrients go, peat is the next thing to a starvation diet, and the other three products add up to zilch. They can be used with the addition of soil, humus or leaf mold.

The pH balance for succulents? Around seven to eight on the scale. However, as the pH scale is figured on the logarithm base of 10 and I am doing well to add two and two, I am not prepared to go any further into it than that.

Cactus/succulent soil has to be gritty! Sounds pretty simple. When people get around to discussing the proportions of the mix, however, the subject can get complicated. There are as many recipes for potting mixtures as there are for the perfect martini, and while everybody agrees on the two basic ingredients, it's the ratio of sand to soil that causes the argument. Once the sand-soil problem has been solved, perlite, charcoal, lime, bone meal, olives and onions can be tossed in as they are needed and according to taste.

Actually, succulent plants are not terribly picky about their soil, and all they want out of their potful is a few vitamins and fast drainage.

This brings us to Rule Number One. Fortunately it is the only rule: Cactus need a heavy, moisture-holding soil like a submarine needs screen doors. And that excludes the generous use of peat, vermiculite and clay. There should be no way you can squeeze a handful of cactus soil and make it hang together. When you open your hand the soil should fall apart. Damp or dry. A gritty, loose texture is what you want. I can recognize the proper soil on sight: If it looks like my aunt's nut-crumble cake it's just right.

YOU GET THREE GUESSES!

There are three ways to tackle the soil mixture problem: simple; easy; and some people never learn!

SIMPLE Buy a bag of succulent/cactus mix! There are several brands on the market, and as far as I can tell they are all perfectly usable. Composition does vary some, so you and your plants may find one preferable to another.

EASY I think this is the best solution as you can vary the sand/soil ratio to suit the species you are potting, and with a minimum of fuss. Buy a bag of regular strength potting soil and a bag of sharp sand. Builders' sand is best; it has coarse, angular grains. These two mixed together anywhere from 50-50 to 25 (sand) and 75 (soil), depending on the individual plant, make a perfectly good medium.

As commercial potting soil often varies greatly, it might be wise to compare package labels. You'll find some that are heavy in the peat moss-clay department; avoid these. Nursery people, by the way, are very impressed by label readers, more so if you thump the bag occasionally and mumble "h'mmm" every once in a while.

Builders' sand, coarse river sand, crushed brick and smashed clay pots are grit. Beach sand is too fine, the grains are rounded and it packs down solid after a few waterings. And no plant appreciates a reproduction of the Daytona Beach Speedway cemented around its roots.

Perlite can be used as a natural grit substitute, but not exclusively. It doesn't provide the bottom weight often needed to keep cactus pots stable and upright. Mix it with some sand or fine gravel. If the white spots of perlite offend your eye, cover the surface with a gravel mulch.

SOME PEOPLE NEVER LEARN If you want to start from scratch and whip up your own bucket of potting soil there are, as I said, innumerable recipes. There is one type I don't recommend. It is usually not found in books, but people do persist in trying it. It is loosely called "the midnight mixture" and it is made up of builders' sand, top-soil, fine gravel and garden humus, in whatever amounts and proportions as can be stealthily gathered from construction sites during the hours of darkness. Due to haste and lack of light, this mixture is unreliable—as may be the consequences to your person if you are not fast on your feet.

The more pedestrian soil mixes are very similar to each other: sand, leaf mold, standard potting soil; sand, leaf mold; and sand, sandy soil, leaf mold.

Experts agree on only one ingredient—sand! They do not agree on how much sand. I'd say for general succulent culture, if the soil is from one-third to one-half sand, you've got it made and there should be no reason to nit-pick about a couple of spoonfuls more or less.

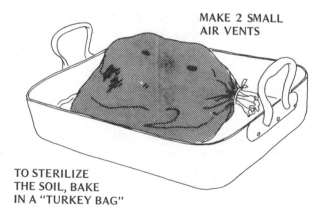

MAKE 2 SMALL
AIR VENTS

TO STERILIZE
THE SOIL, BAKE
IN A "TURKEY BAG"

At first glance it looks like the experts agree on leaf mold, too, but if you delve into it you'll find dissension in the ranks. One says,"Well-composted oak leaf mold is best." Another, with just as much authority says, "Don't use oak leaf mold; it is too acid." Some cactus people who don't want to get into it refuse to designate any particular tree or leaf. They simple recommend some type of humus, or even a good grade of packaged potting soil as a substitute, a position with which I tend to agree.

If you have not been discouraged, and have stirred up a sand-humus-soil mixture of dubious proportions, you are probably wondering what else, if anything, is supposed to go into it. Take your pick of any, all or none of the following.

Charcoal A sprinkle per pot keeps soil sweet, but if the soil is good and gritty, and drains rapidly, it won't have the chance to turn sour.

Bone meal A pinch or two per pot. This is the safest type of fertilizer for most slow-growing succulents. (I ran across one mixture that called for hoof and horn grist. Why does it sound so much more grizzly than bone meal?)

Dolomite lime Maybe a half teaspoon in a six-inch pot, to keep the soil slightly alkaline and counter-act those oak leaves. Or try a few crushed oyster shells, or use the water your hard-cooked eggs were prepared in. Ground mortar from old bricks works, too, as does pulverized concrete, but before you start ripping up the sidewalk, try some easier ways. White-haired or white-spined cactus like an extra shot of lime in their soil, so for them you can nearly double the amount needed for the others.

Fine gravel A handful or two for sharp drainage, if the plant and pot are large. Some species appreciate it even when they are small.

MULCHES

The consistency and color of a rock or gravel mulch is a matter of taste. Shocking-pink aquarium gravel will do the trick if all you need is something to keep the base of a rot-prone cactus from moldering away, but there are other materials more suitable to the plant and to your senses. Light shades of natural colors (gray or beige) are most often used because they harmonize with any plant, pot or decor, and they also reflect both sunlight and collected heat up towards the plant. Stark white does a good job of reflecting, but it tends to be overpowering, and after a few waterings it usually looks dirty.

Angular gravel, rounded beach or river pebbles, and packaged rock from nurseries can be utilized as pot-toppers. Whatever type you fancy should be rinsed well before using; dirt, excess dye and sea salt will do nothing to insure an attractive and healthy plant.

Beware! Rocky mulches can make it difficult to determine the moisture content of the soil underneath. It is often better to wait until you are used to the watering demands of a particular species before adding a decorative or protective mulch.

BE ON THE LOOKOUT FOR . . .

Lately I've seen some large succulents in the supermarket which appear to be planted in pre-stressed concrete. They look like a Mob reject . . . you know, the cement-overshoes-trip-to-the-East River thing. Curious as to what this material was, I took one of the plants and pounded on the "soil" with the store vegetable sprayer until I broke through the crust. (I have also been thrown out of places other than supermarkets.) The pot was filled—to the very brim—with very coarse grit and sand, and the top inch had fused into a solid crust. Water would have run off over the sides before it had time to penetrate.

The plants looked healthy enough, but I doubt if a prolonged existence sealed off by a crust on top and a plastic container on the sides would keep them that way. If you do buy a plant potted this way, either repot it right away or at least chip out the crust, until you can move it to better quarters.

Another lamentable fact: The tags on these plants were not what you could call a bundle of information and they were all identical. "Cactus. Water bi-monthly." The pots held three different genera of cactus, a crassula and an aloe! If I were any one of them, I'd be terribly insulted.

potting

The pot is crocked. The soil is ready. The plant is waiting. All you have to do now is put them all together. If your waiting plant is a spiny cactus, you may be considering the possibility of getting slightly crocked yourself. A surprising number of cactus, however, can be cradled in the hands without any damage to you or it. Give the spines a few tentative pats and find out if it is one of the tame ones. If it has long sharp spines that are spaced far apart, you can usually get a two- or three-fingered grip in between them. If there is just no way you can get hold of the cactus barehanded, pull on a pair of gloves or wrap something around the plant, such as a folded paper or a piece of cloth.

The first experience with cactus potting is usually easy and painless, because our first cactus is more than likely a small one. When they are little and weigh only a few ounces, they can be hand held. Just don't squeeze!

Opuntias require special handling, no matter how small they are. Gloves or a suit of armor is an absolute necessity. Enclosing the cactus in a plastic bag works, too. Pop one over the plant before you take it out of the old pot and don't take it off until it has safely been replanted. A few spines may poke through, but the glochids will stay put. If you want to brave it with gloves, don't wear a soft cotton pair. Hard-finished cloth, smooth leather or plastic coated, if you please. Glochids will stick to soft fabric gloves or suede leather, and three days later when you finally get around to removing your gloves from the middle of the dining room table . . . gotcha!

Smooth cactus and other non-agressive succulents can be handled just as you would any other plant, as long as you remember not to use a viselike grip on them.

Before potting a succulent, check for dead, broken or bruised roots. If there are any, trim them off. Left as is they will probably rot and take healthy roots along with them.

THE EIGHT-STEP PATH

(1) Dump some soil into the pot on top of the crocking.

(2) Set the plant on it and check to see that the "neck" (point at which roots and stem meet) is about one-half inch below the rim of the pot. A

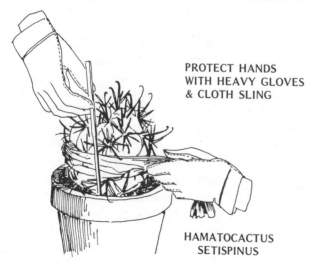

PROTECT HANDS
WITH HEAVY GLOVES
& CLOTH SLING

HAMATOCACTUS
SETISPINUS

little more, if you are going to add a rock mulch.
(3) If necessary take the plant out and either add or subtract soil until it is at the right level.
(4) Hold the plant steady and spoon more soil around it.
(5) Do not tamp the soil down hard. Poke it very lightly with a chopstick, pencil or finger. Or thump the pot down on the tabletop once or twice to settle the soil.
(6) Spread a layer of mulch if you wish. And it's a good idea. It serves two purposes: keeps moisture away from the vunerable neck area of the plant and helps reflect light and warmth. The latter is why commercial cactus mulches are usually white or light in color, although there is no reason why you can't use darker gravel or pebbles if you want.
(7) If it's a tall cactus you might want to wiggle it gently to make sure it's steady and is not going to flop over when you move the pot.
(8) Don't water it!

Yes, I know! Other plants get a good soaking right after potting, but succulents don't need it. Give them a few days to get their roots in working order. Extra moisture in the soil can encourage rot, so it's safer to withhold the initial watering for a while. Most soil mediums, whether home mixed or store bagged, are slightly damp to begin with, and for succulents that is enough for the time being. Of course, your bag of soil may have been left open since last year and is now as dry as a mummy's elbow. What about that? Dampen it very lightly and evenly before putting it into the pot. If you can do it the day before potting, even better.

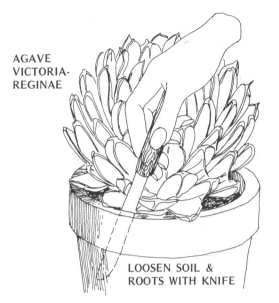

AGAVE VICTORIA- REGINAE

LOOSEN SOIL & ROOTS WITH KNIFE

NEVER PUT OFF UNTIL TOMORROW . . .
Luckily most cactus don't need to be repotted often; between two and six years is about average. If you have a really huge cactus to repot, I have three words of advice, "Put it off!" If it's an opuntia, I have three more, "Give it away!"

Repotting a large cactus can be fraught with difficulties, and I'd certainly try to topdress one with a couple of inches of new soil to forestall a change of pots. But in the event that the pot is cracking open from errant roots, or the plant has bogged down from lack of room, it must be moved to larger quarters. You may need to enlist the help of some friends. Large cactus can be heavy!

Before the operation begins, it is best to wrap the whole plant with padding. Newspapers will do, but they are sometimes hard to tie down. A few layers of material (old sheet pieces, maybe) wound

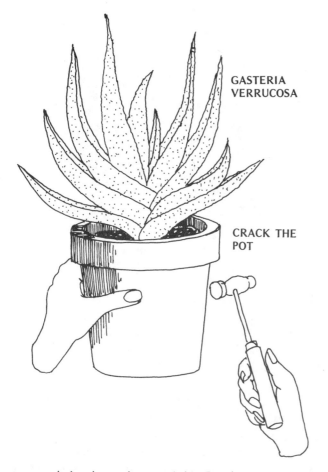

GASTERIA
VERRUCOSA

CRACK THE
POT

AND THEN THERE'S . . .

Cactus aren't the only ones that are tricky to repot as large specimens. Some of the other succulents have very wicked spines. Toothed aloes are no fun. Agaves are in a class by themselves! Watch out for your eyes when you bend over an agave, as the spines on the ends of the leaves can be long, sharp and nasty. Wear gloves and a tough, long-sleeved shirt. If the leaves are limber or flexible enough, tie them up with a soft cord or strip of material to make a smaller and less lethal package, even if it's only enough to get some of the bottom leaves out of their horizontal position. If you don't you are not only going to have a terrible time getting it out of the old pot, but you are going to wish you had never been born when you try to get it into the new one.

WHEN ALL ELSE FAILS

Getting any large, root-bound plant to let loose of its pot often calls for strange feats of manual dexterity, and even stranger vocabularies. Fortunately, the gritty potting soil succulents prefer makes it a little easier to remove the root ball. But don't count on it. If there are more roots than soil in the pot, you may still have trouble. After a few experimental prying, prodding and shaking attempts, if nothing happens, break the pot! And next time don't plant something directly into your priceless Ming vase.

Smaller pots with plants lodged firmly in them can be dealt with in the time-tested manner: Turn the pot upside down and rap it smartly on the edge of the table. It's easy to tell which people have tried this strategy with prickly cactus . . . they are the ones with the bandages on their feet.

around it do a better job. Don't use anything fuzzy, or you'll spend the winter picking lint off the spines. If the plant is a tall, branched one, a few braces might be tied to it to prevent the arms or joints from breaking off.

If this sounds like a lot of trouble, just be thankful you're not moving a 40-foot Saguaro. Professional movers of these monsters use bales and bales of straw and dozens of mattresses for padding. It makes rummaging around for an old sheet seem like child's play.

GOOD, BAD AND UGLY

Some people don't mind the look of red clay pots. In fact, they like 'em. Others would just as soon have a live tarantula in their parlor. There is nothing in the world wrong with giving a pot a slipcover job or a cache pot, if you observe some "buts."

An ornate pot may look great by itself, *but* it could overpower a plant and detract from them both. You can put a utilitarian pot inside of a more pleasing container, *but* make sure there is air space between them, not only for the sake of air circulation and moisture dispensation, but to make sure you can get the inner pot back out again. With a skintight fit, both pots may have to be broken—along with your heart.

Use that fancy bucket to hide a tacky pot, *but* don't forget to put something into the bottom of it to lift the planted pot away from any water that might collect down there. Three or four screw on-type bottle caps work fine for a pot that isn't heavy enough to squash them. A couple of wood strips, or anything else that will raise the inner pot about a half inch, will do. Don't use a solid piece of material right under the drain hole; it's there to drain, not be plugged up. Even after taking these precautions it is wise to occasionally lift the inner pot out and take a look into the cache pot, just to make sure everything is dry down there. Stagnant water gets smelly, and besides that, who needs malaria?

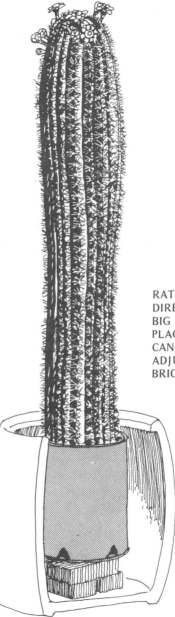

RATHER THAN POT DIRECTLY INTO A BIG CONTAINER, PLACE NURSERY CAN INTO POT, ADJUSTING HEIGHT WITH BRICKS

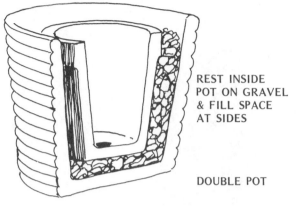

REST INSIDE
POT ON GRAVEL
& FILL SPACE
AT SIDES

DOUBLE POT

SOME CHEAP COVERUPS

If you'd like to cover some of your pots, but can't afford to buy another container at the moment, or ever, try baskets. They look great with most succulents and don't interfere with the necessary air circulation. Fit a saucer into the bottom of the basket so it won't leak.

TOOLS OF THE TRADE

There are only three tools necessary for potted plant culture. Fortunately, they have been scientifically designed and tested so you need have no fears about their usefulness. You shouldn't even have trouble collecting them. They are: one bent fork; one spoon (if money is no object, two spoons); and one chopstick (although most people don't have just *one* chopstick).

When I say bent fork, I don't mean the one you jammed into the garbage disposal. This thing has to be bent in a certain manner. Use an old fork or one from the junk store. Hold it right side up and bend about a half inch of the ends of the tines until it looks like a little rake. Unless you have a grip like King Kong, use pliers and do one tine at a time. This handy tool can be used for everything from leveling to loosening topsoil, raking rock

mulches and sculpting dish garden hills. It is also good for scratching between your shoulder blades.

One spoon is adequate, but it's nicer if you have a big one and a small one. Again, use old kitchen-table utensils; measuring spoons will not let the soil "pour" off. I like to spoon the soil around plants at potting time because you can put it just where you want it without getting pieces of dirt and grit caught in spines or hair. Soil particles behind radial or interlacing spines are hard to remove. Blasting at them with water often pushes them in deeper into the spines, although it will dislodge the particles in some cases. You will have to cover the soil though, before you try this; succulents do not like to be watered when newly potted. It's easier to keep the plant clean in the first place. Use a spoon.

The chopstick? There is nothing better for general poking and prodding, for settling soil around roots and propping up a freshly potted plant until its roots get a good grip. Poking around the roots with a metal tool can do real damage; wood is much safer, but please remember to use a light touch.

Additional tools: Some people use tongs and some don't. I don't. There are other ways to outwit a spiny cactus. I've seen tongs used to the disadvantage of the cactus too many times—broken and bent spines. Broken spines do not grow back. If you want to try them, go ahead, but be very careful, and use padding. It doesn't take much pressure to get spine-crushing leverage. Or bruising. You will also need a clean, whistle-sharp kitchen knife for making cuts on the plants, such as at grafting time, and you may find shears or pruners handy for trimming roots (never stems as they may be crushed).

water

"Don't water on rainy or overcast days."
"When in doubt, don't water."
"Don't water more than twice a month."
"Don't water in winter."
"Don't overwater."

Sound familiar? Much of the popular advice given boils down to "don't." It's enough to give people a complex. In fact, it has; some people are afraid to water their cactus. Growers who give them too much water are about equal in number to those who give them too little.

Starting at the top of the "watering advice" list, let's take them on one at a time.

DON'T WATER ON RAINY OR OVERCAST DAYS

Where I live, in the Puget Sound area of the Pacific Northwest, I could stand around with my watering can for three months waiting for a sunny day ... in the summer. The local weather forecast goes like this: "If you can see Mt. Rainier, it will rain within eight hours. If you can't see it, it's already raining." So, during the growing period (spring and summer) if my succulents need water, I give them water.

If your climate has a more balanced share of sun and cloud, then do try to water on the bright days. Sunshine does discourage lingering moisture in the soil, especially on the surface where it can start a damaging rot. (A rock mulch helps keep the base of a cactus dry, in cloud-country locations.) But, suppose your growing, flower-forming cactus

has held down the fort for a long, hot weekend while you were away, and now that you're back you can see that the poor thing is parched. You grab the watering can, and the clouds roll in. Somewhere in the back of your mind a little voice says, "Remember, don't water on rainy days!" Tell that little voice to take a hike, and water the plant.

WHEN IN DOUBT, DON'T WATER

This is actually a good piece of advice for growers who have tended other plants, but are trying out their first cactus. Letting the soil go almost or completely dry between waterings takes a little getting used to.

"When in doubt ..." means if you are not sure the plant needs water today, then do it tomorrow. It does not mean that you can be doubtful until the middle of next week, or next month.

DON'T WATER MORE THAN TWICE A MONTH

This statement is way too broad! Watering depends on too many ifs and buts. Twice a month may be fine for a large plant, but I see the same printed instruction on little ones that don't measure an inch in any direction. Just where is a tiny cactus, in a little pot, sitting in the hot sun, expected to store two weeks worth of moisture? For a couple of months in the summer these babies may need to be watered every day.

Forget the bi-monthly bit and water when the soil ball is as dry as each particular plant wants to be. And according to size, species and location, this can take anywhere from one day, to one week, to every second passing of Halley's Comet. Do not let the soil remain dry for more than a day or two when the plant is actively growing and blooming. At this time, succulents need more water than most people think they do.

DON'T WATER IN WINTER
In the first place, how long is your winter? And what kind of winter? Rainy and gray? Foggy? Snowy? Mild? Three months winter and nine months poor sledding? By the way, how long does a succulent think winter is? That's who we are concerned with here!

Winter for a succulent is between two and three months, no matter how long yours is. During that time it does not want frequent watering, but for a potted specimen, *no* water at all is ridiculous. All cactus/succulents need *less* moisture in the winter than they do in the summer, usually a lot less. Check big ones every two weeks and little ones every week. It the plant begins to look dull and shriveled, water it lightly; a dormant plant does not want to be soaked.

Winter watering should be just enough to keep the roots from drying to a crisp, but not enough to induce growth. If there are any signs of growth, move the plant to a cooler place if you can and hold back the water. Dormant means a complete standstill, but a healthy one . . . not a setback. Its appearance should not change, for better or worse.

Usually, the cooler a plant is kept, the deeper the sleep and the less water it takes. And of course size makes a difference, too: Small, thin-stemmed or leafed succulents will shrivel much more quickly than a large, bulky barrel type. To keep them on an even keel, you can't stick them in a corner for the winter and forget them. That's why I suggest taking a look at them every week or so.

DON'T OVERWATER
What constitutes overwatering? It amounts to giving succulents another drink before the last one is used up.

Just before an overindulged succulent rots off it will begin to look soft and fat, with an unhealthy, translucent color to the skin, like somebody who has dropsy. Once the patient is this far along, nothing short of a miracle will cure it. Keeping it warm, semi-shaded and completely dry may revive it, but the chances are mighty slim.

Overwatering, for desert cactus and most other succulents, is a continually damp soil. If you are watering often enough to keep this much moisture in the pot it is too much. Let it go dry and start over again.

A CRASH COURSE IN NATURAL DRINKING HABITS
The best thing you can do for a succulent is to try to duplicate its natural cycle as closely as possible. Watering *au naturel* can be overdone. Getting a subscription to *The Dry Gulch Gazette* from Arizona and watering only when the weather column says it has rained in the desert doesn't work. By natural, I mean thinking about how the water cycle works. If you understand *how*, the *when* almost takes care of itself.

Like any other plant, each succulent has its own definition of "dry," ranging from barely to bone, but most of them are not particular about the finer points. A few of them are, and when a succulent is classified as *difficult* it means the plant is touchy about the time lag between its wet and dry periods. It needs a careful balance, which is sometimes hard to discover.

One thing they all agree on is that they *hate* a stingy drink. When it rains in the desert, it *rains.* A deluge, a downpour. The same type of rainfall is experienced by succulents growing in places other than the desert. Succulent plants have adapted themselves to collect water, store it, use it, and then wait for more. It louses up the internal machinery if more moisture is added while they are still collecting the last batch. With a built-in survival reflex, impossible to turn off, succulents will try to absorb *all* available moisture. If there is too much, too soon, they will literally drink themselves to death.

When you water a succulent, do it generously. Wet the entire root ball. (After a semi-dry winter, you may have to soak plant, pot and all to accomplish this.) Throughout the growing season, drench the plant, let it go dry, then drench again.

It often pays to find out what the mature size of a cactus is. That two-incher may be a seedling, or it may be a senior citizen, full sized and better able to bear the burden of hot sun and drier soil.

MORE OR LESS

Succulents can take more water when they are:
- Thin leafed or stemmed, flat padded, many branched, or small.
- In small or flat, shallow containers.
- In porous containers.
- Growing, budding, or flowering.
- In a hot, sunny location.
- Root bound.

Succulents need less water when they are:
- Large barrel or ball types, or thick columnar ones.
- In glazed or plastic containers.
- Resting.
- Large and bulbous rooted.
- In dull and cloudy weather.
- Newly potted.

One definite "don't": Don't use cold water. Slightly warm, please! How would you like it if you were enjoying a sunbath and some fool sneaked up and threw a bucket of cold water over your lower extremities? Well, it's a terrible shock to plants, too.

fertilizer

DESERT CACTUS

When the subject of fertilizer comes up, some growers say "yes," some say "no," and some of us just sit around looking blank—through no fault of our own. It doesn't make for a lively discussion, although the subject does lend itself well to some rather colorful language.

Those authorities who say "yes," say it with certain reservations, and *if* you can stay within their guidelines, ok; otherwise, it could be a disaster. You can improvise and experiment with other cultural precepts, but *this* is no place to be creative. Follow the rules!

• It must be a formula low in nitrogen. Fertilizers with a high nitrogen content produce quick, lush growth . . . hardly a cactus' style.

• It should *never* be applied in the fall or winter. Don't fertilize a dormant, or going dormant, succulent of any brand.

• Applications should be well diluted, moderate and given about once a month during the growing season.

• Slow-release fertilizers, of the right nitrogen content, are fine, providing they are applied only *once* in the spring. One dose will last for the entire growing season.

• Caution is advised in the use of fish fertilizer; over a period of time it can become toxic to some succulents.

Now is the time to sit down and have a good, honest talk with yourself; if you think you will be tempted to do *more*, then don't fertilize at all. Your cactus will be infinitely better off! The wrong type, or too much of any fertilizer, will not hurry these plants along or force bloom. All it will do is inspire some goofy, soft, stringy, undesirable stems and shoots—or kill. Cactus can't be pushed into growing faster, bigger and better. Feedings are meant to maintain healthy, natural, and often slow, growth, not screw it up.

THE ALTERNATIVES

Bone meal in the potting mix is an easy and safe way to boost both soil and plant. Repotting fairly often will also keep a plant in victuals. Very little pots run out of nutrients quickly, about once a year, but if the occupant is growing steadily, wait another season before giving it fresh soil; it's still eating well.

OTHER SUCCULENTS

Large or vigorous succulents, aloe, agave, yucca, some of the epiphytic cactus and other fast growers or heavy bloomers, will welcome a monthly feeding throughout their growing season. Small, slow-growing ones should be treated delicately as the desert cactus.

light

Trying to grow a desert cactus in poor light is about as rewarding as investing in buggy whip stock. Some of the other succulents may like the shade, but desert cactus need sunshine. Most of them need all they can get; six hours a day is ideal for best growth and bloom. If you can't get that kind of mileage out of old sol, four hours will usually still do the trick.

If your summers are 90° F plus, some protection from the afternoon sun is appreciated by all but the very large plants. The tops of the cactus don't mind the heat, but the roots do. Yes, yes, I know the temperature of the dessert floor often goes up to 150° in the summer, but, 18 inches down in the ground it is only 60°. And unless you have a very large plant in a very large pot, there is no 18 inches down for a house plant. What you usually get after several hours in broiling sun is a bad case of "hot pots." And fricasseed roots! This "hot pot" condition is another reason why tame cactus need more water than their wild kin.

Especially in the winter, a surprising amount of light can be lost due to dirty windows. Smoke film, especially, builds up slowly and evenly, unnoticed until it gets to the stage where you could view a solar eclipse without risking your eyes. If your plants begin to look a little puny, and you are wondering why nobody else has complained about having 17 days of fog, it might be wise to wash windows.

A cactus will grow without its full quota of sun, but it probably won't bloom. I can't say it *definitely* won't bloom, because as soon as I did 50 people would come out of the woodwork clutching cactus plants that have bloomed in the broom closet. Let me put it this way: *As far as anybody knows*, sunlight is essential if you want flowers.

If the cultural instructions for a plant say, "partial sun," give it morning sun and skip the rest of the day. If it's "no direct sun," keep it out of the blaze, but give it a brightly lit location; the plant did not request a dark corner.

Succulents may be fond of heat and sun, but they resent poor air circulation. They do not like a stuffy, poorly aired room. Fresh air, not a cold draft, will do much to perk up their spirits, and keep bug infestations at bay. Mealy bugs and spider mites love warm, dry, stale-aired plants.

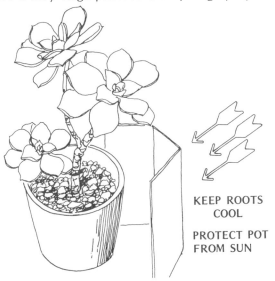

KEEP ROOTS COOL

PROTECT POT FROM SUN

summer and winter care

SUMMERING OUT

Like many other house plants, succulents enjoy a summer vacation out of doors, especially cactus. But while cactus can tolerate blazing sun and extreme heat in their native habitat, as captive potted plants they need some relief. Put them where they will have good air circulation and, depending on your climate, either filtered sun or full sun for only part of the day. If your summers are very hot give the plants full sun until around noon and light shade for the rest of the day. Water them thoroughly and often; they will dry out much faster than they do in the house. If you live in an area where summers are moderate and often interrupted by showers, give your cactus full sun and protect them from overwatering due to rain. For instance, if it rains for a week in mid-July, move the pots to a sheltered spot until the monsoons let up, then move them back out into the sun.

Non-cactus succulents? The same drill, except for those few that do not like full sun whether inside or out. When in doubt, place outdoor pots under the mottled shade of a leafy tree, or the diffused light of an awning or slatted patio roof.

Bring everybody back in when nighttime temps dip toward 55° F, and give them a cool place to rest for the remainder of the winter.

WINTER CARE

What's with these succulents and their mysterious cool, dry dormant period? Nothing really, it's just the way they were brought up. All plants rest; succulents are more diligent resters, that's all. And in order to do it properly they like a lower temperature and less water. Nothing strange about that. Would you go happily off to bed if someone plunked you down in front of a warm fire and plied you with food and drink? I hope not!

IS THIS TRIP NECESSARY?

Many cactus growers remove their plants to a porch, basement, cold frame or attic for the winter. But, what if you don't have any of those places? Maybe you don't even have a cooler, unused room, like an extra bedroom or something. Then what? Well, my succulents stay in the same room year around: spring and summer in the sunniest window; fall and winter about four feet to the left on the floor just below the window, and out of my heater's reach. Because of some tender tropicals growing in the same room, the thermostat is set for no lower than 60° F, but over in the cactus corner 60° it ain't.

A minimum of 45° to 50° F is cool enough for most cactus, although some of the mountain types can take it much colder in the wild. Fifty-five degrees is plenty low enough for the warmer-growing species. Next time you don't have anything else to do but walk around the house kicking furniture, find a thermometer and test the temperature in a few places around the house. Seek places that have good light, with or without direct sun. By or below a window, away from furnace registers, radiators or other sources of heat, are usually the best bets. If your pots end up right next to a window, and your winters are the below-freezing type, you may have to have some nighttime protection, such as a sheet of paper or a curtain, between plant and glass. The temperatures up close to a frosted window can become mighty brisk!

In the fall, move your plants to their "cooler place" and start slacking off with the water; let the drier periods become longer and longer. If the plant has to go on the wagon, then it should taper off. No "cold turkey" treatments.

WHAT TIME IS IT REALLY?

Some plants from the extreme parts of the southern hemisphere have a little trouble with jet lag; when it's winter here, it's summer there. These plants may want to take their nap when everybody else is waking up. Some will become acclimated, others won't. (Many lithops and other mesembs grow according to their own time zone, come hell or high water.)

Before you add a new succulent to your collection, find out if it is one of these turned around plants. It could save the plant's life, and your sanity. Plants running on southern time will show signs of growth in the winter, probably even blooming at that time. In the summer they often shrink down into the soil and snooze so effectively that uninformed people have tossed them out, thinking they were dead.

THE REDCOATS ARE COMING!

Some of the best cactus books are written by English authors, and the books are quite naturally meant for English growers. Many of these books are enjoying popularity in the United States, however, and growers here may notice some differences in the winter culture sections. Some of the authors mention these differences and others don't.

English winters are gray, cloudy or foggy, cool and damp. The average home is not kept as warm as ours is, as central heating is not as widespread. Consequently, the air is not as dried out. Result? Their cactus can go longer without water than ours can. It is not unusual to find the notation, "Older plants must be kept completely dry from the beginning of November until the end of March." In our warmer homes, a five-month winter drought is too long.

In this country the advice is, "*Move* the plants to a cool location." English growers advise a cooler spot, too; they just don't mention *moving* anything. "At coolish *room temperature*," they say, "about 60° F, but not below 54°." Many Americans are appalled at the English custom of drinking beer at room temperature, but if the suds are kept next to the cactus pots, room temperature beer would be fine with me.

By all means, read the books. Most of them are excellent. But follow the watering advice with discretion, remembering that the English grow cactus at cooler temperatures than we usually do.

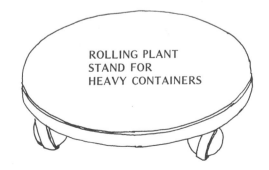

ROLLING PLANT
STAND FOR
HEAVY CONTAINERS

communicating with your cactus

All green thumb people like to talk about their plants. Some of us like to talk *to* them. Within the last few years scientists have accepted the fact that a little conversation is a good thing for all concerned. Succulents are no different from other plants in this respect. They respond to people who talk to them.

When you have an extra minute, have a chat with your cactus. Actually, there is no one like a cactus to tell your troubles to; even better than a bartender. They have had more problems than anybody and are quite understanding. How can you lay your troubles on a leafy, nervous tropical who is already a temperamental basket case? For weeks after you'd feel guilty every time a leaf fell off.

If you don't feel like talking, all plants like music—almost any kind, it seems. But I don't think any plant appreciates the "1812 Overture" played at window-rippling volume, with the possible exception of an Artillery plant. Any tremendously loud music seems to make plants nervous. No fooling! It can vibrate their leaves right off. I've never had the spines fall off a cactus after a blast of crescendos, but they definitely had a pretty loose hold on them and they looked exhausted.

Quite a few young people bring me sick plants; not diseased, not overwatered or underwatered, not mispotted, just sick. Headache probably. I've found they usually revive nicely by just giving them a little peace and quiet.

insects and disease

PREVENTION

Although succulents are seldom attacked by bugs and blight, they are not completely immune. Poor air circulation, sloppy watering and other bad cultural habits can pave the way to several problems. Bugs usually don't bother a well-tended, healthy plant, but a flabby, uncared-for one is like an invitation to dinner. The best way to avoid an invasion is to keep everybody clean and healthy.

TAKE ANOTHER LOOK

Sick plant? Before you hit the panic button and drag out an assortment of noxious sprays, inspect the plant very closely; make sure you really have insects. There is a good chance that you don't. An improper cultural condition may be the cause of the sickness. Unless you can actually see little creatures walking around, your first consideration should be to find out if something else is wrong.

• Brown or gray corky patches on the lower stem of some cactus is a natural aging trait that some people mistake for a mysterious disease.

• Pale, elongated growth is a sign that the plant is not getting enough light or sun. Move it.

• No new growth? Usually either worn out soil or too much water. Repot and water more carefully.

• Yellowish leaves or stems? Could be your plant is too dry, too stuffy and too hot. Give it some air, less roasting in the sun and a little more water.

• If you are not getting any flowers, read the label on the bag or bottle of fertilizer again; it may contain too much nitrogen. The plant also might not be getting its prescribed winter rest. Consider what you did last year and make some changes.

• Soft, bloated growth is caused by too much water or low temperatures during the growing period. Reduce water and move the plant to the warmer place.

• A glassy look in the winter? Probably frostbite. If the whole plant is affected, it will not survive. Minor damage will leave lasting scars, but the plant will not die. Keep plants away from very cold or frosted windows.

NONE OF THOSE THINGS?

Ok. Maybe you do have a buggy plant. First thing to do is move it away from any other uninfected plants before you get a general trend going. Then look for one of the following.

• *Fuzzy, white mealy bugs* Pick off with a toothpick or dab with alcohol. If plague proportions, a spray of nicotine sulphate can be used.

• *Aphids* Small sucking insects from pale green to black in color, usually found on tender new growth. Some distortion of new growth will be evident. Wash plant with soap and water, dose insects with an alcoholic Q-tip, or use nicotine sulphate spray.

• *Red spider* Unless you use a hand lens you won't be able to see these little devils, although their fine webs are usually visible. A reddish smudge on your finger after touching the underside of a leaf or stem will tell the tale. Yellow or white spots on leaves will be your first clue. A few soap and water baths should clear them out. Dry, stuffy rooms are very inviting to red spiders.

• *Scale* A brown, hard-shelled insect which attaches itself very firmly to the plant, and is undisturbed by a bath unless you really scrub. They can be pried off with fingernail or toothpick, but be careful of bruising the plant.

Almost all insects can be beaten down with a sudsy bath or two, and a little diligent toothpick work. As far as I am concerned, sprays are strictly a last resort remedy. If you do have to use them, follow the instructions to the letter and do not use any product containing Malathion if members of the crassula family are present: kalanchoe, cotyledon, echeveria and the like.

Systemic insecticides work well for all sucking insects. They are put into the soil and absorbed by the plant, making any bug bite a lethal one. There are several good systemic products on the market, complete with instructions for their use. Read them and don't guess.

WHAT YOU'VE GOT THERE IS A CASE OF ROT

Overwatering, bruising, unhealed cuts and open wounds are the main reasons decay strikes a succulent. And most of the time these conditions are brought on by sheer carelessness. Fungus infections bide their time, until the door is left wide open by some negligent succulent grower. There is no cure; infected parts must be removed.

If the base of the plant is stricken, the top can be cut off and re-rooted. Throw the bottom part away and wash your hands before handling the healthy section.

Spots of rot on stems should be cut away, down to good tissue, and dusted with a fungicide (like Captan). Leaves with decay should be cut off and tossed out.

If your succulents show an inclination for rotting, heed the warning: The air is too humid, you are knocking the plants around too much, or you are not watering them properly. It has to be one of them.

seeds

Many succulents grow easily from seed. Propagation from seed is the slowest means for any plant, and for some succulents it is a *very* slow way. This method, therefore, is not for everyone, but for some of us it is very satisfying and our "from seed" plants mean twice as much to us as the ones we bought half grown.

SOIL MIXTURES

I suppose all of us have a favorite potting-soil recipe that we will gladly speak up for. Most seed growers have a secret, never-fail seeding mixture that they will defend to the death! In locked rooms, they stir up combinations of vermiculite, sand, peat moss, leaf mold, perlite and pulverized brick. I have a hunch some commercial seed sowing mix is sneaked in, too.

Funny thing about it is that almost any mixture will do the job. The most important factor is the care of the seeds after planting, not the soil. A bag of pre-mixed, commercial seeding medium will suit the purpose.

SOWING THE SEED

Fresh seed is best for germination and sellers of packaged seeds usually try to make sure you are getting the good stuff. (Seed packets are also often dated by the manufacturer.) But, as with any seed, not every single one is going to sprout. The most interesting for beginnners are the packets of mixed species; most of us wouldn't know what to do with 187 rebutia seedlings anyway.

Spread the soil mixture into fairly shallow pans or containers, with holes in the bottom. Seed trays, plastic or waxed cartons from the kitchen or low pots will do. Seeding soil should be as sterile as possible, but if you want to play it really safe, a fungicide for damping off (like Captan) can be sprinkled on.

Large seeds should be pushed gently into the soil until they are just below the surface. Small ones are scattered over the top and left alone. Warning! Some succulent seeds are minute and dustlike. One good healthy sneeze while sowing and you'll be out of business. These tiny fellows will also appreciate a thin sifting of peat to sit on; they can get lost in the larger particles of regular soil. Using a flour sifter (if you can get away with it) or a sieve, put a small amount of peat over the top of your filled container.

Now, if the soil is not already damp, soak the planted container from the bottom in a pan of warmish water until it is moist clear through. Moist, not soggy. And keep it that way.

The best way to maintain moisture is to put the container in a plastic bag, or under glass. Germination depends on a damp, warm soil. If it looks like it's drying out while you are waiting for sprouts to appear, soak it from the bottom again.

Most succulents germinate best at 70° to 80° F. If you can't supply some artificial heat under a plant light or with a soil cable, put the seed pans where they will get strong window light and warmth, but no sun. Plant in late spring, when the

PUSH LARGE SEEDS
GENTLY BELOW SURFACE

USE A FLOUR SIFTER OR FINE
STRAINER TO SPREAD A THIN
LAYER OF PEAT OVER SEEDS

IMMERSE IN LUKEWARM WATER
TILL THOROUGHLY MOIST

MAKE A FOLDED PAPER
TUBE TO HOLD & SCATTER
VERY TINY SEEDS

ENCLOSE MOIST CONTAINER
IN PLASTIC BAG & KEEP WARM,
GIVE STRONG NATURAL OR
ARTIFICIAL LIGHT. VENTILATE
AFTER FIRST SIGNS OF GER-
MINATION

weather will cooperate. With a controlled heat source, you can plant earlier. I get off to an early start by putting my seed pans on top of the hot water heater.

SEEDLING CARE

Germination takes place anywhere between two days and a month, depending on the species. Some succulents can hardly wait, and some like to mull it over for a while. Be patient and don't give up.

After the seeds have sprouted, ventilate them every week or 10 days by opening the bag or removing the glass for an hour or so. If your seedlings are a mixed bag, you will notice that some of them have definite cotyledons (two immature leaves), while others look like little green balls right from the start. Seedlings are ready to come out from under their greenhouse in three to six months, but keep them out of direct sun for the first year.

Succulent seedlings are usually left in the same germinating pots or pans for about a year, unless there is very tight crowding. Transplant carefully; their roots are fine and fragile.

158

cuttings

Most succulents are very easy to root; it's part of their survival plan. In fact, some of them don't know when to quit! They will produce material for cuttings from leaves, parts of leaves, stems, sections of stems, pieces of branches, and parts of the flowering stem. Not to mention offsets, new crowns and small shoots.

No plastic tents or glass jars are needed or wanted. Do not cover succulent cuttings. They need fresh air, warmth and good bright light (no direct sun). The best time to take cuttings is in the spring when plants are putting forth their maximum growth.

THE ROOTING MEDIUM
Any sandy, well-drained rooting mixture will do, home mixed or commercially bagged. Do-it-yourself types recommend: three parts sand to one part loam; half sand and half perlite; or equal parts peat, perlite and vermiculite.

Whatever you use, keep it loose, porous and sandy. Don't pack it down. Firm it up with a few gentle pats or one thump on the table. Any container with holes in the bottom will do; it does not have to be deep. Succulent cuttings are not buried in the soil. They are either planted very shallowly or just placed on top of the soil. If the cutting has any height to it, it will have to be propped up.

FIRST AND FOREMOST
Before potting, all succulents must be callused off. Pereskias are the only exception. After taking the cutting, lay it someplace where it's warm and shady until the cut end looks dry and filmed over with a callus. Without this drying period, the cutting will rot when it is put in contact with the damp rooting soil. How long a cutting takes to callus depends on how big the cut surface is: a day for a thin stem or leaf edge, a week or two for a large chunk of cactus. No specific number of days can be given; when the end looks dry, it's ready. If "ready" day also happens to be the day your vacuum cleaner blows up or the stove shorts out, the cutting will be happy to wait until a more convenient time rolls around. A day or two extra does not spell doom for a succulent.

THE MOST DRASTIC CUT: COLUMNAR CACTUS
Large columnar cactus are sometimes lopped off, beheading it's called, because they have gotten too tall for their surroundings, or because the grower wants the cactus to keep a full head of white hair going. It takes a lot of nerve to cut it off in the first place, and even more to wait through the callusing period, but the chances of failure are not great. After the end has dried (and it takes a long time), set it on the rooting soil and prop it with a tripod of sticks. Rocks shoved up around the bottom of the plant can cut off good air circulation and hold moisture. Soil should be barely moist. Root development on large cuttings can be horribly slow; be patient. If there are any signs of softness or rot around the cut end, chop it off, dry

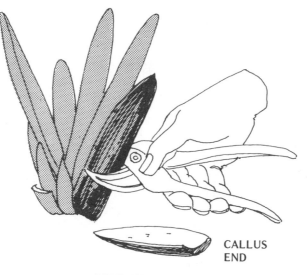

CALLUS
END

LEAF CUTTING

again and replant. Might be a good idea to dry it a little longer this time.

Don't throw away the bottom part, the stump, of the cactus; it will usually sprout a whole gang of new columns on the edges of the old one. These can be left to grow as is, or cut off when they are a couple of inches long and rooted.

Large stem cuttings can be made from other succulents, too, but the sections must have leaf nodes on them. These are the slightly raised areas on the stems from which leaves and branches grow. The procedure is the same; cut, callus and plant. The old stem will resprout.

LEAF CUTTINGS
Many plants with fleshy basal leaves, like the *Gasteria*, can be propagated from small sections of a leaf. Cut a leaf from the plant, slice into pieces horizontally, mark the top side, let dry and insert into rooting soil right side up.

Use a whole leaf with attached stem for others, such as crassulas and kalanchoes. Place a knife against the stem of the plant on the upper side of a leaf stalk, then cut down about a third of the way through the stalk. Gently tear it the rest of the way with your fingers, to get the bud at the base of the leaf. Callus and plant.

Leaf cuttings can be taken from echeverias using the same technique, or the top of the plant can be cut off and rooted. The old stem will produce offsets which can be twisted off, dried a bit and rooted in soil.

Many rosette-type succulents will not only propagate from leaves, they will do it from pieces of the flower stem. Cut one of the long stems into sections of two or three leaves each, callus briefly (not long for these thin stems) and plant; be sure they are right side up.

BRANCHING OR SEGMENTED STEMS

Opuntias and epiphytic cactus have a growing form which makes it very easy for propagators. There are also branching cereus types and euphorbias and other succulents that grow in a segmented fashion. Sections for cuttings are simply removed at a ready-made joint. Protect your hands for the removal of an opuntia pad, then carry on as usual. Some jointed or branched cactus are very loosely put together and obtaining material for propagation consists of picking broken stems up off the floor. If one of this kind gets bumped too often, you could end up with more cuttings than plant.

OFFSETS

Clustering succulents, cactus or otherwise, are the easiest to propagate of all. Many times the small offsets will already have roots, and these can be carefully pulled off and potted without further ado. Rootless offsets should be cut off with a sharp knife and given the callusing treatment.

NOTE

Succulent cuttings, of any kind, can be dusted with a hormone product such as Rootone to stimulate root growth. Apply it when ready to plant, dusting cut end of cutting only.

NEVER-FAIL TECHNIQUE . . .
WELL, HARDLY EVER

(1) Remove desired section or leaf.
(2) Callus off in warm, dry, shady spot.
(3) Dust with Rootone or other hormone product.
(4) Set on rooting soil, or plant very shallowly.
(5) Prop if necessary and place in warm, airy, well-lit location with no direct sun.
(6) Keep soil barely moist and do not cover.
(7) New growth on plant means that roots have formed.

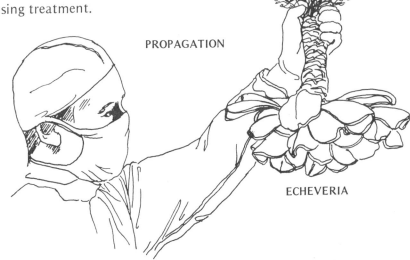

PROPAGATION

ECHEVERIA

161

grafting

Cactus grafting is more complicated than the other forms of propagation, but it is not nearly as exacting as the grafting processes of other plants. Why graft? There are several reasons.

• Some cactus do not do well on their own roots when they are potted because the exact natural requirements of their culture are too difficult to duplicate indoors.

• Grafting will preserve fasciated or crested oddities, and the strange little plants with no chlorophyll of their own, such as *Gymnocalycium* cultivars.

• Many grafted plants will grow more vigorously than they would from cuttings.

• Because of earlier mistreatment, roots are sometimes damaged to the point where grafting will revive the plant quicker than trying to re-root it.

• Some people just like to experiment, to see if they can make two plants look better than one.

• Some plants branch more freely on a grafted "stock" than on their own roots, therefore more cuttings can be obtained.

Not all succulents can be grafted. Cactus, euphorbia and milkweed family members, which have an inner growth ring, or cambium, take to it very well. The best time for the operation is during the spring and summer when the plants are growing strongly.

The bottom plant is called the "stock" and it should be a sturdy specimen which grows well and has no quirky root problems of its own. The top piece is the "scion" and it can be any graftable species that will fit onto the bottom plant.

Cleanliness is very important; keep the cut ends dirt free, and use a clean, very sharp knife for cutting.

Cactus spines are often used to hold the plants together until the graft takes. They are pushed through the scion and stock at an angle to "pin" the pieces together. They will eventually dissolve and leave no trace. Toothpicks and pins can be used, but they will leave small scars and pins may also leave rust marks. Some scions are held on with string or rubber bands, going around the pot and over the top of the plants. If you use rubber bands, make sure they are just barely stretched. Too much pressure and you're going to have a pretzel. A little pad of tissue or cloth can be used under the string or bands, to protect the top of the scion.

There are three types of grafting cuts: *flat*, for rounded scions; *cleft*, for flat ones; *side*, for the long and slender.

FLAT

This type of graft, fitting two flat pieces together, is the easiest. Slice the top off of the stock plant, then make another, very thin slice and leave it on, to keep the surface moist and clean. Trim down the edges, or shoulders, of the plant with slanting cuts. If left flat, they can push the graft off.

Slice off bottom and trim the edges of the scion in the same way as the stock. If one plant is

162

bigger than the other on the outside, it doesn't matter, but the inner growth rings must match up. If you weren't right with the first cuts, slices can be taken off either piece until you get a match.

Remove the protective slice from the stock and without wasting any time, apply the scion and press them together. Gently! Just enough to make a good contact and exclude any air. Fasten the whole thing together with rubber bands and leave it for about two weeks in a warm, slightly shaded place. A moderate amount of sun won't hurt, but it doesn't want to be fried.

When the two weeks are up, very carefully remove the rigging and gently touch the scion to see if the graft took. If it didn't, start over again from the beginning, making new cuts. If it did, it's ready for regular cactus culture.

CLEFT

Using the same procedure, cut a shallow "V" in the stock and a wedge shape to fit the "V," in the scion. The two pieces can be tied with string or fastened with a few cactus spines. After-graft treatment is the same as above.

SIDE

Instead of both pieces being cut flat, they are slanted; otherwise the procedure is the same all over again. Be sure the scion is well fastened, or it may have a tendency to creep off.

NOTE

Do not let moisture, from sprinkling, watering or whatever, collect on newly grafted plants. Those edges you trimmed back are very susceptible to rot, until they have had time to heal over. Water as usual for species.

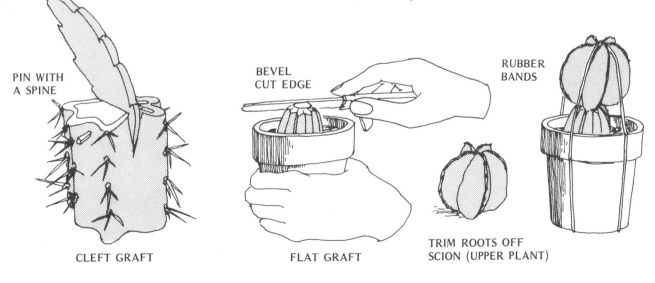

PIN WITH A SPINE

CLEFT GRAFT

BEVEL CUT EDGE

FLAT GRAFT

TRIM ROOTS OFF SCION (UPPER PLANT)

RUBBER BANDS

mail-order source list

Abbey Garden
Toro Canyon Road
Carpinteria, CA 93013
cactus/succulents; $1 for catalog

Ashwood Specialty Plants
4629 Centinela Avenue
Los Angeles, CA 90066
succulents; 25 cents for catalog

Arizona Cactus Farms
Box 249
Superior, AZ 85273
cactus/succulents; 25 cents for
  species list

Beahm Epiphyllum Gardens
2686 Paloma St.
Pasadena, CA 91107
epiphyllum; 35 cents for catalog

Cactus by Mueller
10411 Rosedale
Bakersfield, CA 93308
30 cents for catalog

California Epi Center
Box 2474
Van Nuys, CA 91404
epiphytes; 50 cents for catalog

Chris and Son Nursery
860 West Columbia Lane
Provo, UT 84601
cactus seed; 25 cents for species
  list

Desert Dan's Cactus
Minotola, New Jersey 08341
50 cents for catalog

Desert Flora
11360 East Edison
Tuscson, AZ 85715
cactus/succulents; visitors and
  inquires welcome

K and L Cactus Nursery
12712 Stockton Boulevard
Galt, CA 95632
75 cents for catalog

Loehman's Cactus Patch
8014 Howe Street
Paramount, CA 90723
30 cents for catalog

Nature's Curiosity Shop
2560 Ridgeway Drive
National City, CA 92050
cactus/succulents, some crested
  and monstrous; 75 cents for
  catalog

Scotts Valley Cactus
5311 Scotts Valley Drive
Scotts Valley, CA 95066

Ed Storms
4223 Pershing
Fort Worth, TX 76107
lithops and other mesembs; 50
  cents for catalog

index

Page numbers in italics indicate
an illustration.

Adromishus festivus, 110
Aeonium, 61-62
  arboreum, 61-62
  arboreum var. *atropurpureum*,
    61-62
  arboreum cv. Zwartkop, 62
  ciliatum, 62
  decorum, 62
  Haworthii, 62
Agave, *8*, 81, 82-84, 150
  americana, 83
  americana cv. 'Marginata,' *80*
  Attenuata, 83
  horrida, 83
  parvifolia, 83
  Patoni, 83
  stricta, 83
  utahensis var. *nevadensis*, 83
  Victoriae-Reginae, 83, *143*
Aizoaceae, 103
Alkaloids, 23, 24
Aloe, *8*, 81, 84-85, 150
  arborescens, 84
  aristata, *80*, 84
  brevifolia, 84
  haworthioides, 84
  nobilis, 84
  nobilis 'Gem,' 84
  socotrina, 84
  spinosissima, 84
  variegata, 84
  vera, 84-85
Aporocactus, *120*
  flagelliformis, *111*, 125
Areole, 18, 28
Ariocarpus, 81, 89
  agavoides, 89
  fissuratus, 89
  fissuratus var. *Lloydii*, 89
  Kotschoubeyanus, 89
  Kotschoubeyanus var. *albiflorus*, 89
  Kotschoubeyanus var. *elephantidens*,
    89
  retusus, 89
  trigonus, 89
Astrophytum, 51-53, 66
  asterias, *46*, 52
  capricorne and cultivars, *14*, 52

  myriostigma and varieties, *46*, 52-
    53
  ornatum and varieties, 52-53
Austrocephalocereus, 67-68
  Dybowskii, 68
  lehmannianus, 68
Aztekium Ritteri, *6*, 118

Baby Burro's-Tail, 61
Baby Joshua tree, 61
Barbados Nut, 116
Bare Foot cactus, 76
Barrel cactus, 22, 39, 99
Bear Feet, 76
Beaver Tails, 91, 93
Bird's-nest cactus, 50, 101
Bishop's Cap, *46*, 52
Boojun tree, 115
Borzicactus, 71
Botanical divisions, 30, 32
Botanical names, general information
  on, 30-36
Branching stems, propagation by, 161
Bulbous roots, 22
Bunny Ears, 91, 92
Burro's-Tail, 61
Bursera, 113, 116
  fagaroides, 116
  gummifera, 116
  microphylla, 116
  Simaruba, 116

Cactaceae, 18, 107
  history of family, 19-22
Cactus, 9-14
  botanical divisions of, 38, 39
  defined, 18
  origin of term, 34
Calico-Hearts, *110*
Callusing, 159
Candelabra plant, 84
Candelilla, 23-24
Carnegiea gigantea, 55-56, *145*
Candy barrel, 99
Cat Claws, 99
Century plant, 83
Cephalium, 28
Cephalocereus, *37*, 67-68
  chrysacanthus, 68
  luecocephalus, 68
  senilis, 68

Cereus, 56
  hexagonus, 56
  Jamacaru, 56
  Jamacaru cv. 'Monstrosus,' 114
  peruvianus, 56
  peruvianus cv. 'Monstrosus,' *54*, 56,
    114
Cereus type, 23, 35, 39, 55-59, 67-71
  monstrous forms, 114
  propagation of, 161
Cespitose, 28
Chalk Lettuce, 78
Chamaecereus, 47, 48, 58
  Sylvestri, *6*, 57
Chamaelopsis, 58
  X 'Fire Chief,' 58
Cholla, 94-95
Christmas cactus, *111*, 120, 121-123
Cinnamon cactus, 93
Cleft-type graft, 163
Cleistocactus, 69
  Ritteri, 69
  Strausii, 69
Columnar cactus, cuttings from, 159-
    160 *see also* Cereus type
Compass barrel, 99
Conophytum, 103, 105
  Elishae, *102*, 105
  Meyeri, *102*, 105
  placitum, 105
  tumidum, 105
Containers, 132-134
  crocking, 137
  hanging, 135-137
  size, 134-135
Coral Beads, 61
Coral cactus, *111*
Coral plant, 116
Corn cob cactus, 59
Coryphantha, 53
  clavata, *14*
Cotyledon, 76, 77
  ladismithiensis, 76
  luteosquamata, 117
  orbiculata, 77
  orbiculata var. *oophylla*, 77
  reticulata, 117
  Ritteri, 6
  teretifola, 76
  tomentosa, 76
Cowhorn, 119

Crassula, 17, 61-62, *74*, 77-78
  arborescens, 77
  aborescens var. *glauca*, 77
  argentea, 62
  argentea cv. 'Crosby,' 62
  argentea cv. *'Variegata,'* 62
  brevifolia, 62
  deltoidea, 77
  X 'Jade Necklace,' 62
  Lycopodioides, *60*, 62
  perforata, 62
Crassula family, effect of Malathion
  on, 156
Creeping Devil cactus, 100
Crests, 114
Cristate, defined, 28, *95 see also* Crests
Crocking, 137
Crown-of-Thorns, 63
Cuttings, propagation by, 159-161
Cylindropuntia, 91, 94-95

Dam's Chin cactus, *46*, 50
Desert cactus, 38, 39
  fertilizing, 150
Devil's Head, 100
Devil's-Tongue, 99
Diseases, 12, 156
Diurnal, 28
Double potting, 145
Dudleya, *74*, 78
  Britonii, 78
  pulverulenta, 78

Eagle Claws, 98
Easter cactus, 122-123
Easter Lily cactus, 48
Echeveria, *8*, *37*, 76-77, 78
  candida, 78
  crenulata, 78
  Derenbergii X 'Doris Taylor,' 76
  elegans, 78
  farinosa, 78
  glauca var. *pumila*, 78
  setosa, 76
Echinocactus, *17*, 34-35, 39, 98
  Grusonii, 98
  horizonthalonius, 98
  ingens, 98
  polycephalus, 98
Echinocereus, 34-35, 69
  Delaetii, 69
Echinolobivia, 47
Echinopsis, *13*, 36, 47, 48-49
  aurea, 48
  Eyriesii, 48
  kermesina, 48
  multiplex, 48
  turbinata, 48

Elephant bush, 63
Elephant tree, 116
Emerald-Idol, 95
Epiphyllum hybrids, *110*, *120*, 126
Epiphytes, 38, 121, 123-124, 126
  culture for, 121-123
  propagation of, 125, 161
Eriocereus, 125
Espostoa, 69-70
  Blossfeldiorum, 69
  lanata, 69-70
  melanostele, 70
Etiolate, 29
Euphorbia, *8*, 23, 58-59, 63, 119, 161
  Bojeri, 63
  caput-Medusae, 119
  clavrioides var. *trucata*, 119
  grandicornis, 119, *128*
  grandicornis cv. *'Cristata,'* 6
  horrida, 59
  horrida var. *nova*, 59
  ingens, 59
  Knobelii, 59
  Ledienii, *54*, 59
  lydenburgensia, 59
  meloformis, 119
  Milii var. *splendens*, 63
  Milii var. *imperatae*, 63
  obesa, 119
  submammillaris, 59
Euphorbiaceae, 58

Fasciate, 29
Faucaria, 105
  lupina, 105
  tigrina, 105
  tuberculosa, 105
Felt plant, 77
Fenestraria, 105-106
  aurantiaca, 105
  rhopalophylla, *102*, 105
Ferocactus, 51, 99
  acanthodes, 99
  corniger, 99
  hamatacanthus, 99
  latispinus, 99
  melocactiformis, 99
  rectispinus, 99
  Wislizenii, 99
Fertilizer, 150
Fire Ball, 99
Fire-Crown, 45
Fishhook barrel, 99
Flat-type graft, 162-163
Flowers, 11
  botanical terms for, 35-36
  of *Stapelia*, 79

Fouquieria, 113, 115
  fasciculata, 115
  Idria columnaris, 115
  Purpusii, *112*, 115
  Sheveri, 115
Fruit, botanical terms for, 36
Fungicide, 156
Gasteria, 81, 88
  Armstrongii, 88
  X *Gasterhaworthia* 'Royal High-
    ness,' 88
  liliputana, 88
  verrucosa, 88, *144*
Gem-tooth aloe, 84
Glochids, 23, 29, 92
Glory-of-Texas, 101
Glossary 27-28
Golden barrel, 98
Golden Old Man cactus, 68
Golden Stars, 50
Golden-tooth aloe, 84
Grafting, 125, 162-163
Gymnocalycium, 49-50, 162
  baldianum, 49-50
  Damsii, *46*, 50
  Mihanovichii, 50
  Mihanovichii var. *Friedrichii*, 50
  Monvillei, 50

Hair, 21
  on cactus, 33, 65-66
  on other succulents, 66
Hamatocactus, 51
  septispinus, *6*, *46*, 51, *142*
  uncinatus, 51
Harrisia, 125
  Bonplandii, 125
  Jusbertii, 125
  tortuosa, 125
Hatiora, 124
Hat-Pin cactus, 99
Haworthia, 87-88
  attenuata, 87
  blackbeardiana, 87
  cymbiformis, 87
  cymbiformis var. *translucens*, 87
  fasciata, 87
  Reinwardtii and varieties, 87, *128*
  setata, 87
  truncata, 87
  turgida, 87
Hedge cactus, 56
Hen-and-Chickens, 78
Homalocephala texenis, 100
Hoya carnosa, *110*
Hylocereus, *120*
  undatus, 123-124

Indian fig, 91
Insecticide, 156
Insects, 12, 155-156

Jade tree, 62
Jatropha, 116
  Berlandieri, 116
  cathartica, *112*
  Curcas, 116
  hastata, 116
  integerrima, 116
  multifida, 116
Johnson 'Paramount' hybrids, 47, 58
Jointed cactus *see Opuntia*
Joshua tree, 85-86
Jumping cholla, 95

Kalanchoe, 77-78
  beharensis, 77, *131*
  pumila, 78
  tomentosa, 77
Kleinia, 111

Lace haworthia, 87
Leaf cuttings, 160
Leaves, 19
Lemaireocereus, 56-57
  Beneckei, 57, 66
  Chichipe, 57, 66
  marginatus, *54*, 57
  pruinosus, 57
  Thurberi, 57
Leuchtenbergia principis, *133*
Light, 151
  for epiphytes, 122
Linnaeus, Carolus, 30
Lithops, 106
  Aucampiae, 106
  Aucampiae var. *Koelemanii*, 106
  Aucampiae var. *kuruman*, 106
  fulviceps var. *latinea*, 106
  optica ruba, 106
Living Rocks, 106
Lobivia, 47-48, 49
  aurea, 47
  cinnabarina, 47
  Hertrichiana, 47
  Higginsiana, 47
  Jajoiana, *46*, 47
  kermesina, 47
  leucomalla, 47
  Pentlandii, 47
  planiceps, 47
Lobiviopsis hybrids, 47, 49
Lophocereus, 70
  australis, 70
  Sargentianus, 70
  Schottii, 70, *133*
  Schottii cv. *'Monstrosus,'* 70, 114
Lophophora Williamsii Lemaire, 24, 25

Machaerocereus, 100-101
  Eruca, 100
  gummosus, 100-101
Madagascar palm, 59
Malathion, effect on crassula family, 156
Mamillopsis, 36, 73
  Diguetti, 73
  senilis, 73
Mammillaria, 23, 39, 50-51, 72-73
  bocasana, *64*, 72-73
  camptotricha, 50
  candida and varieties, 72
  discolor cv. *'Cristata,'* 114
  elongata, 50
  elongata cv. *'Cristata,'* 114
  fragilis, 50
  gracilis, 50
  Hahniana, 73
  plumosa, 73
  Schwarzii, 73
  Sheldonii, 50
  Wildii, 50-51
  Wildii cv. *'Cristata,'* 114
  Zeilmanniana, 51
Medicinal properties of succulents, 23
Medusa's-Head, 119
Melocactus, 34
Mescal, 24
Mescaline, 24
Mesembryanthemaceae, 103
Mesembryanthemum, *33*, 103-104
Mexican Fence Post, 57
Mexican Firecracker, 76
Mexican Sedum, 61
Mexican Snowball, 78
Milkbush, 119
Mini Jade, 62
Mistletoe cactus, 124
Monstrous forms, 114
Moonstones, 79
Mother-in-Law's Seat, 98
Mulches, 141, 143
Music for succulents, 154

Naming of succulents, botanical, 30-33
Night-blooming cereus, 22, 123-124
Notocactus, 53
Offsets, 29
  propagation by, 161
Old Lady cactus, 73
Old Man cactus, 68
Old-Man-of-the-Mountains, 71
Opsis, defined, 36

Opuntia, 23, 29, 39, 73, *90*, 91-95, 97, 161
  articulata, 94
  basilaris, 93
  Bigelovii, 95
  clavarioides, 95
  cylindrica, 95
  cylindrica cv. *'Cristata,'* 114
  diademata, 94
  Engelmannii, 93
  erinacea, 73
  Ficus-indica, 91
  floccosa, 73
  fulgida, 95
  inermis, 92
  leptocaulis, 95
  megacantha, 91-92
  microdasys, 92-93
  microdasys var. *albispina*, 93
  monacantha, 92
  rufida, 93
  Salmiana, 95
  strobiliformis, 94
  Tuna cv. *'Monstrosus,'* 114
  Turpinii, 94
  Verschaffeltii, 95
  vestita cv. *'Cristata,'* 114
  vulgaris, 92
Opuntia Tephrocactus, 94
Orchid cactus, *110*, 126
Oreocereus, 71
  Celsianus, 71
  fossulatus, 71
  Ritteri, 71
  Trolli, 71
Organ-Pipe, 23, 39, 57

Pachycereus Pringlei, 56
Pachycormus, 113, 117
  discolor, 117
Pachyphytum, 76, 79
  oviferum, 79
Pachypodium, 59
  Lamieri, 59
  Leadii subsp. *Saundersii*, 59
Pachyveria, 76
Panda plant, 77
Parodia, 53
Partridge-breasted aloe, 84
Peanut cactus, *6*, 39, 57
Pebble plants, 33, 106
Pedilanthus, *8*
Pencil cactus, 95
Pereskia, 107, *108*, 109, 159
  aculeata, 109
  aculeata var. *rubescens*, 109
  Bleo, 109

167

Godseffiana, 109
grandiflora, 109
sacharosa, 109
Pereskiopsis, 36, 109
velutina, 109
Peruvian Old Man cactus, 69-70
Peruvian tree cactus, 56
Peyote, 24, *25*
pH balance for succulents, 138
Pilocereus, 67
Pilosocereus, 67, 68, *96*
flavilanatus, 68
Palmeri, 64, 68
Royenii, 68
Pincushion-type cactus, 39 *see also*
Mammillaria
Playtopuntia, 91-93
Pleiospilos, 106
Bolusii, 102, *106*
Nelii, 106
Popcorn cactus, 124
Portulacaria, 63
afra, 63
afra cv. *'Tricolor,'* 63
afra cv. *'Folius Variegatis,'* 63
Potting, 142-143
double potting, 145
epiphytes, 122
repotting, 143-144
Pots *see* Containers
Powder-Blue cereus, 57
Powder Puff cactus, *64,* 72
Prickly Pears, 91, 92
Princess-of-the-Night, 124
Propagation
from cuttings, 159-161
of epiphytes, 125
grafting, 162-163
from seed, 157-158
Pseudo, defined, 36
Purple and Powder plant, 78

Rainbow bush, 63
Rattail cactus, *111,* 125
Rebutia, 42, 44-45
albiflora, 45
calliantha, 45
grandiflora, 45
Marsoneri, 44, 45, *133*
miniscula, 44, 45
muscula, 45
pulvinosa, 45
senilis, 45
violaciflora, 45
xanthocarpa, 45
xanthocarpa salmonea, 45
Red-Crown, 45
Repotting, 143-144

Rhipsalis, 36, 124
baccifera, 124
Cassutha, 124
cereuscula, 124
mesembryanthoides, 124
pendula, 111
Ribs, 21, 22
Rice cactus, 124
Root systems, 22
Rosette form, 81
Rot, 12, 156

Saguaro, 23, 55-56, *145*
Sansevieria trifasciata cv. *'Laurentii,'*
111
Schlumbergera, 120, 123
Bridgesii, 123
Gaertneri, 123
truncata, 123
Sedum, 8, 61
amecamecanum, 61
confusum, 61
Morganianum, 60
Morganianum cv. 'Baby Burro's-
Tail,' 61
multiceps, 61
X *rubrotinctum,* 61
Sieboldii, 110
Stahii, 61
Seeds, propagation from, 157-158
Segmented stem cuttings, propagation
by, 161
Selenicereus
grandiflorus, 23, 123-124
pteranthus, 124
Sempervium arachnoideum, 110
Senecio Rowleyanus, 111
Shark's Jaw, 105
Side-type graft, 163
Silver-Beads, 77
Silver Torch cactus, 69
Snake plant, *111*
Snake's-Head, 119
Soapweed (small), 86
Soil, 138
for epiphytes, 121
for potting, 139-140
for seed sowing, 157
Soft-tip yucca, 86
Spines, 21, 23, 34
Split Rocks, 33, 106
Stapelia, 79
Desmetiana, 79
gigantea, 79, *136*
grandiflora, 79
variegata, 79
Starfish Flower, 79
Stem cuttings, propagation by, 159-160
segmented, 161

Stomata, 21
Stonecrop, *110*
Strawberry cactus, 51 *see also*
Hamatocactus septispinus
String-of-Pearls, *111*
Succulents, defined, 18
Summering out, 152

Talking to succulents, 154
Taproots, 22
Taxonomy, 30
Teddy Bear cactus, 95
Tephrocactus (Opuntia), 91, 94
Texas Horse Crippler, 100
Thanksgiving cactus, 122-123
Thelocactus, 96, 101
bicolor, 101
bicolor var. *tricolor,* 101
lophothele, 101
nidulans, 101
Thimble cactus, 50
Thrixanthocereus, 69
Tiger aloe, 54
Tiger's Jaw, 105
Tools, 146
Totem Pole cactus, 114
Tree aloe, 84
Tubercles, 21, 29

Uebelmannia, 118
pectinifera, 118
pectinifera var. *pseudopectinifera,*
118

Watch Chain, *60,* 62
Water, 10, 147-149
for epiphytes, 122
Wax plant, *110*
Wilcoxia, 71
Schmollii, 31, 71
senilis, 71
Window plants, 22, 87, 105
Winter care, 152-153

Yellow Torch cactus, 68
Yucca, 22, 81, 85-86, 150
aloifolia, 86
brevifolia, 80, 85-86
elata, 85
elephantipes, 86
glauca, 86
gloriosa, 86
recurvifolia, 86
pendula, 86
Whipplei, 86
Yucca Cane plant, 86

Zygocactus, 35, 123
truncatus, 123